Pig Moments
God Moments
to Remember

Dr. Keena K. Cowsert

Foreword by Sue Thurston

Pig Moments: God Moments to Remember
Copyright 2018 by Keena K. Cowsert
ISBN 978-0692184417
ISBN 0692184414

DK Community Publishing
Keena K. Cowsert Press
PO Box 1642, Sarasota FL 34230

Website: www.*DKcommunity.org*
Email: *info@DKcommunity.org*

Cover Design by Bonnie Joy Kelley of BonFire Ministries
Edited by Jeanne Bardel and Ann Gervasio
Text Dividers by Freepik.com

Printed in the United States of America

ACKNOWLEDGEMENTS

Honor and praise to Jesus for always seeking me out and coming after me, even when I was distant from Him. Thank you, Holy Spirit for the work you have done on the inside of me!

To Bonnie Joy Kelley for coming along side me the past two years in unbelievable ways. Your life sets an example for me every day. You have been the calm voice through some of life's storms this past year. Your words of encouragement have built me up and taught me how to encourage others. Partnering with you in ministry has been a JOY and I am honored to call you friend. And thank you for a beautifully designed cover!

To Michelle Skorski for accepting this conservative girl onto your team. The Front ministry has been so instrumental in creating an environment of freedom allowing me to go deeper with God. I love running with you on this journey, as we partner to do Kingdom work. I am honored to call you friend.

To my friends, Candy Pfeifer, Jennifer Passmore, Dianne Steele, Carol Burton, & Mike and Ann Gervasio who read this book and encouraged me that others would be touched by its content.

To Cameron Scott Cowsert for being part of my story!

PRAISE FOR

Pig Moments:
God Moments to Remember

Keena's insight, open mind, search for something more, and accurate self-evaluation has placed her on a spiritual fast track to revealed truth from the scriptures and hearing from God. This book will encourage you to know that you are not isolated in your weakness and guide you toward restoration, healing, and wholeness. One of your personal "Pig Moments" will be the epiphany that God is no respecter of persons and what He is doing in Keena's life He will do for you!

> ~ Candace Pfeifer
> The Pfeifers

I was so encouraged as I read Keena's story! We overcome by the blood of the Lamb and the word of our testimony (Revelation 12:11). Watching her personal growth and journey has been such a delight. God really is on the move and He is drawing us with His kindness. Pig Moments will help you put the spotlight on your own heart, allowing God to bring healing in any broken areas and reflect on all that He has done for you. Take these personal reflection opportunities and invite Him to do a deeper work in your heart and in your story as well. There is always more of Him!

> ~ Michelle Tellone-Skorski
> The Front

PRAISE FOR

Pig Moments:
God Moments to Remember

This book is a living, breathing example of how God, His Word and His people, work in the heart and mind of someone to change them. People often ask me how to grow in their faith and relationship with God. This is an intimate look in to how it happened for Keena and how you can apply what she has learned to your own life.

~ Jennifer Passmore, Pastor's wife

In this book, Keena has taken off the mask and shown her vulnerability to stir in me my own. She has written with such openness and depth that each section ministers to my heart. Keena's humility and honesty has allowed me to fill in my own blanks.

~ Carol Burton

These God-Stories will bring up times in your life you thought you had already dealt with, only to realize there is more to surrender. They encourage you in your life path to enjoy the God Moments and bring healing, too. I definitely recommend them in your life journey with HIM.

~ Ann Gervasio
3 Strand Creations Web Design

FOREWORD

Pig Moments and God Moments ……. You have heard it said, "never judge a book by its cover." When I first heard of Keena's newest book, Pig Moments, was the moment I heard that familiar saying and wanted to add, "never judge a person by their cover." Covered she was…covered by fears, insecurities and questions.

Keena and I met two years ago at a ladies meeting. She stood back and observed me, being sure to keep her distance. She came to hear me speak again, but left early trying to shield the women with her, from some "radical passionate woman." That was me! A few months past, and wanting to "not judge me by my cover", she comes to hear me speak again. At the end of the meeting, we engaged in a personal conversation. I recall her story of all the "kids" in her life. I later learned she had fostered, which still amazes me to this day. Several months later, we met again at another ladies' ministry gathering. Shortly after, she calls to invite me to speak at a women's conference she was hosting that fall. That began our journey together!

As I began to read the manuscript of "Pig Moments", I heard an old song I can remember singing in the church back in the 80's…. "It is joy unspeakable and full of glory, oh. the half has never yet been told!" Keena describes her God moments, "JOY, rolled down window moments", through her journey up the mountain of her personal transfiguration. They will have you recalling, or maybe for the first time realizing, your own personal ones.

I encourage you write them, journal…Psalm 90:12 tells us by numbering our days we gain a heart of wisdom. It is with Joy that you will draw water from the wells of salvation (Isaiah

12:3). You might find yourself holding your head out the window of life with some "wheeeeeees". I have seen Keena have "wheeeeeee" moments" and those be the joy of her heart, that draws from the wells of salvation for her every need.

Your words were found and I ate them, and Your word was to me the joy and rejoicing of my heart; For I am called by Your Name, O Lord God of hosts (Jeremiah 15:16). I have seen Keena eat and consume the Words of God, and watch it change and fill her life with Joy. I watch her as she comes fully into her inheritance as a daughter of the King. She now wears His name so boldly and joyfully.

In Matthew 15:21 his Lord said to him, *"Well done good and faithful servant; you have been faithful over a few things, I will make you ruler over many things. Enter into the Joy of your Lord."* Keena has been and continues to be faithful over the few and the many things. She is ruling over things that used to rule over her life (insecurities, fears…and the list goes on). Her servanthood in the body of Christ has allowed her to enter in to her Lord's Joy.

My prayers for all who read this book, is found in Isaiah 61:1-5. I am praying the anointing on this book, will bring the good tidings, heal your broken hearts, bring liberty to the captives of your heart, and open the prisons of your soul. May the words comfort you and help you see the beauty in your own ashes and bring you the oil of Joy and a new garment to cover you, one of Praise and Joy!

P. Sue Thurston,
Arise and Thresh International Ministries

TABLE OF CONTENTS

TABLE OF CONTENTS

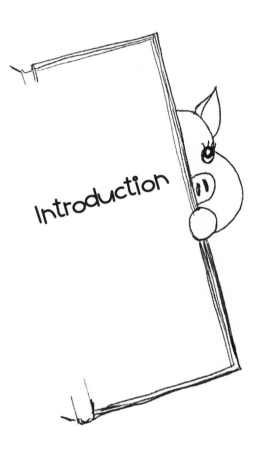

Introduction

INTRODUCTION

Wheeeeeee.....

Remember the childhood nursery rhyme, *This Little Piggy* by Herman:
> *This little piggy went to market,*
> *This little piggy stayed home,*
> *This little piggy had roast beef,*
> *This little piggy had none,*
> *And this little piggy cried "wee wee wee"*
> *all the way home.*

There was also a commercial with a pig in a car with his head hanging out the window yelling Wheeeeeee, Wheeeeeee, Wheeeeeee all the way home. Well, I feel a bit like that pig. This last year has been the ride of my life. Like the pig, I just want to stick my head out the window, feel the wind in my hair and let out a Wheeeeeee.

Too often we fail to recall all the God moments in our lives. When they occur, we feel like yelling out Wheeeeeee or saying, "Thank you God for what you are doing." Yet, too soon we forget that moment. Some of us may journal and some of us may not. Journaling certainly can help us to remember what God has done and is doing in our lives. Yet, from day-to-day, we often live as though we have forgotten His faithfulness to us.

This book is about His faithfulness to me. I will share the many *Pig Moments* in my life over the last two years. The times when God showed up in such a huge way that it left me saying, *Wheeeeeee*. My prayer is that it helps you to remember those moments in your own life. I pray this book inspires you to start writing down what God has done for you and through you.

He does miracles in all our lives and we need to make sure, we do not overlook them. The miracles and God moments not only make our faith stronger, but they may also give someone hope for his or her own life. Write them, type them or speak them into the voice memo on your phones. Just document them to honor and thank God and to strengthen your faith and hope in the Lord.

Before telling you more about my "Pig Moments", let me set the stage by giving you some background.

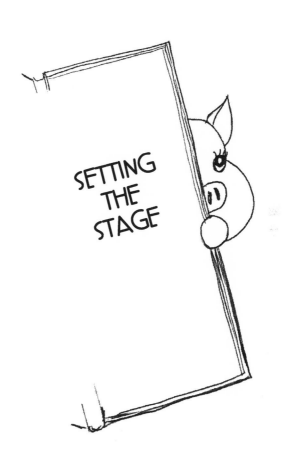

SETTING
THE
STAGE

SETTING THE STAGE

At the age of eleven, I asked Christ into my life as Lord and Savior, so I have been walking with Him most of my life. Just like in your life, there are ups and downs, mountains and deserts, triumph and defeat, joy and sadness, and peace and unrest. Since we are not made perfect at salvation, we each walk out many of these paths during our lives. There are stages and phases we each experience. Some are based on our physical age, some on life circumstances or even our spiritual walk. In our lives, things come and go, cycle, re-cycle, dissipate, enlarge, and so on. Each step of our lives known by God before we were even in the womb (Psalm 139:17) and knowing He set a plan for us (Jer. 29:11).

If you had asked me a year ago about my walk with Christ, I would have told you that I know and love Him and do my best to follow Him. After all, I know many scriptures, all the basic Bible doctrines, and have led several ministries. I had been faithful to my church for the past fourteen years and loved and supported my pastor and his wife. So, everything was going along well. I led a women's ministry and it was growing. The team of women I worked with were incredible and life was good . . . . . or was it?

Our women's ministry team organizes an annual two-day conference and some one-day mini conferences. One of the intentional things we do at each event is to invite outreach organizations from our local area to be a part and to showcase those ministries. We have ten to twelve groups at each conference. Groups like Umbrella Women, Florida Baptist Children's Homes, Hope 4 Communities, Special Needs Prom, Samaritan's Purse, West Florida Foster Care Services, Solve Maternity Homes, Care Net Crisis Pregnancy Centers, Child Evangelism, GRIP, and more.

Things are going along well, and the ministry is growing. Along comes a rocky road that shifts everything. The ministry that is thriving is becoming too much for the church to handle. Staff changes come, and we are asked to take the women's conference elsewhere. That seems reasonable since our team had morphed into a group of women from about eight local churches. However, the other side of me liked the comfortable atmosphere I had grown accustomed to over the years. It was bitter-sweet to make this change. It was necessary, and God was already opening doors. Yet there was a feeling of loss as well.

At different stages in our lives, God begins to shift and move each of us outside of our comfort zone. It is not surprising, He would shift our women's group too. We started the necessary paperwork to become a non-profit organization and began visiting other churches as possible venues for our annual Daughters of the King Women's Conference. We were just in the beginning stages of trying to figure out what to do and how to begin when I received a call from Pam Hawn, inviting me to coffee. Pam leads Hope 4 Communities, a local non-profit organization that ensure homeless and needy children have what they need for school each year and even provide health check-ups and other services. God had given Pam discernment that something was shifting in our situation. She wanted to talk to me about the organization, Galatians 6:2 (G62). It is an umbrella organization for other ministries that need a 501(c)3. Her non-profit organization had been under G62 for some time and she suggested I talk to them before doing this on our own. I gave her several reasons why I did not think that was a good idea, but she was insistent and made me commit to call them. With a sigh, I agreed to do so. After a few weeks of seeing the note on my desk, I finally sent an email and scheduled a meeting with Gary Crawford at Galatians 6:2 (www.G62.info).

Three of us from our women's ministry team went to meet with Gary at their building, King's Station. We felt the Holy Spirit's presence from the moment we entered the building. Not to mention, we are Daughters of the King and we are meeting at King's Station. God is so cool!

Over the past several years, our team had been working to build community, by knocking down the denominational lines to bring women in our community together. Gary's organization was doing the same on several fronts in our community. We felt unity of spirit and purpose almost immediately. God had given him the vision to create this organization to bring local non-profits together and to be able to provide some services for them, if needed.

One thing Gary said to us was that it was sad that our church had not come along side us and commissioned us to go forth. He was so right! It seems churches can become so caught up in running the business side of the church that they forget to develop and commission new ministries. God tells us to "*go into the world and preach the gospel*", yet some churches are too busy managing a budget, staff, activities, ministries, etc. God was moving us to something new, something more community based, something more grassroots. That move was to become part of a group with unity of spirit and vision for our commUNITY. Without hesitation, DK Community, became an affiliate under Galatians 6:2.

In the meantime, God was moving us into new arenas. In late November 2016, we were asked to move the ministry out of the church and by January 2017, we already had four new events scheduled in four different venues. We hosted an Art Gala in February, a one-day mini conference in April, a leadership training in May and a Women's Night of Worship in July. So, God had enlarged our territory already with four events we had never done before. God had been moving very intentionally in the ministry and now He was about to shift His focus to me.

Michelle Tellone, a local radio personality from The Joy FM, was a speaker for our first conference in 2013. In October 2016, at a Joy FM concert, I saw Michelle. I asked her to speak at our 2017 event, which was more than a year away. She said yes, and we agreed to talk after the first of the year. She and her husband lead a ministry called The Front, and it just happens to be about two miles from my home. I needed to connect with Michelle about the fall conference and she said she would be at The Front. So, a Monday night in March, I decided to meet her there and stay for the evening to check out their ministry.

And thus, begins the Pig Moments . . . . . .

Pig
Moment 1

BE STILL
and
LISTEN

Pig Moment 1
BE STILL and LISTEN

It is late March 2017, and I wandered into The Front on a Monday night, having no idea what to expect. The Front is a local ministry that has a weekly service with worship and a speaker. It is held on Monday nights because they do not want to compete with the local churches. This ministry began as an outreach to the younger generation and has transitioned over the years to a wide span of ages and backgrounds. On any given Monday night, there will be pastors and ministry leaders sitting next to ex-addicts, prostitutes, and homeless who have wandered in off the streets. It reminds me a bit of how the Brooklyn Tabernacle started. The Front organizes many street and community outreach events. You may have something similar in the town you live in.

My motivation that first Monday was to see Michelle, but I loved the entire atmosphere so found myself back there the next several Mondays. I have always loved music and worship, as it sets the atmosphere for a service or event. I try to be lost in the worship, but my type-A self often has trouble turning off my thoughts. It seems like satan will do whatever he can to disrupt pure worship.

At The Front, they take time with each song rather than moving from song to song, as if on a tight schedule. They follow the Holy Spirit's lead. They may spend ten to fifteen minutes on one song, just allowing us to marinate in the words, waiting on God to move in lives and hearts. It is all about setting the atmosphere to connect with the one true God in a very personal way. Coming from a conservative and somewhat rigid background, I found the freedom refreshing.

The third week I went, something changed in me and I will never forget March 27, 2017. That night the worship went for over two hours. As the song *In Your Presence (Jason Upton)* was being sung, the words went straight to my heart.

> *"Father I am waiting, I need to hear from you. To know that you're approving, of what I say and do. Cause nothing really satisfies like when you speak my name.... In your presence, all fear is gone. In your presence is where I belong."*

I closed my eyes and just focused on Him. I was able to focus on worship, just being present, and not letting my mind wander. For the first time, I focused about ninety percent of my mind and spirit on worship. That is really good for a type-A, multi-tasker who needs to keep her mind busy. God allowed me to be in His presence without all the distractions and it was opening my heart in a new way. I was at a place in my life where I so needed to hear from God. I thought I needed answers, but what I really needed was just to be in His presence.

The very next song was *No Longer Slaves (Jonathan David & Melissa Helser)*. Again, the words pierced my heart.

> *"You unravel me with a melody, you surround me with a song."*

That was exactly what God was doing. He was unraveling me, peeling back the layers through song and worship. I felt Him so near, so lovingly breathing life into me. The lyrics continued,

> "... till all my fears are gone. I'm no longer a slave
> to fear, I am a child of God."

As the words encompassed my heart, God started to show me fears in my own life. This startled me! I have always been assertive (too much for the liking of some) and never really thought of myself as fearful. Yet, God was playing out before me, fears in my life that were keeping me from truly surrendering to Him.

I have always blamed my social awkwardness on my introverted personality. I am not much of a hugger and do not like large social gatherings... ok to be honest, I do not like most social gatherings. While completely comfortable on a stage talking to a thousand people, I am terrified of being at a social event with twenty people I do not know. God was showing me my insecurities and telling me that introverted or not, I did not have to FEAR. He went further to show me how I keep a distance in relationships out of FEAR of being hurt. How I am a perfectionist out of FEAR of not being accepted. How I tend to critique everything, out of FEAR that I do not measure up. So, as you can see, this is a lot to take in for someone who thinks she is fearless.

In that two hours of worship, I felt His presence so near and so comforting that it was indescribable. Being still and focusing every ounce of my attention on Him, opened my ears to hear Him and my eyes to see myself and Him more clearly. Even though He had opened my eyes to things I had ignored, I felt loved, not condemnation.

> *There is no fear in love; but perfect love casts out fear: because fear hath torment. He that fears is not made perfect in love.*   I John 4:18

> *Fear not; for I am with you: be not dismayed; for I am your God: I will strengthen you; yes, I will help you; I will uphold you with the right hand of My righteousness.*   Isaiah 41:10-13

As we grow in a love relationship with God, His love neutralizes the fears that hold us captive or paralyzed us. Perfect love makes us FEARLESS and faith is the process of walking out that perfect love, so we can unlearn the irrational fears.

That night as I walked to my car, I felt overwhelmed by His presence and love. Unable to drive, I sat in the parking lot and called my friend, Bonnie Joy Kelley. She walks so closely with God that you can feel His presence when you are with her. Through the tears, I tried to describe what God had just shown me. I had such peace … peace into the depths of my soul. This was the first *"pig moment"*. I just wanted to yell out to the world how great He is. I wanted to roll down the windows and *"wheeeeeee"* all the way home.

God was showing me how to just be present with Him. He was showing me how to be still and be in His presence, so I can hear His voice. He was saying to me, "STOP and be still. Listen and I will speak."

REFLECTION

Be Still and Listen

Sitting still may be one of the hardest things for us. If you are like me, as soon as you sit down, you think of ten other things that need to be done. Suddenly, a drawer you have not cleaned out in years, must be done right then. Our culture does not value sitting still or being quiet. The media keeps us bombarded with messages on the radio, TV and social media. Even when we do sit down to "chill" and watch a bit of TV as a family, everyone in the room is also on their cell phones at the same time. It is no wonder we can no longer focus our minds..... we are showered with constant messages.

God seems to have taken second, third or fourth place in our lives to all the social media outlets. It would be enough to just check Facebook, but then we also must check Twitter, Instagram, Snapchat, and keep up with whatever iMessage games we are playing. I wonder how often God is knocking on our heart's door and we cannot even hear Him because of all the noise and distractions. How many times has He been speaking to us, and we cannot hear Him? He created us because He wants a relationship with us, yet we are too busy with things designed to pull out attention elsewhere. Do not think this is by accident. The enemy is smart, and he has used technology to keep us too busy for God. It is time to STOP. Time to be still and quiet before our God.

Take time to read the passages in the Bible that admonish us to *Be Still, Be Quiet,* or *Rest*.

Psalm 46:10
Be still and know that I am God.

Psalms 37:7
Rest in the LORD, and wait patiently for Him.

Psalms 62:5
My soul, wait thou only upon God; for my expectation is from Him.

Psalms 91:1-16
He that dwells in the secret place of the most High shall abide under the shadow of the Almighty.

Isaiah 32:17
And the work of righteousness shall be peace; and the effect of righteousness quietness and assurance forever.

Habakkuk 2:1
I will stand upon my watch, and set me upon the tower, and will watch to see what He will say unto me, and what I shall answer when I am reproved.

REFLECTION QUESTIONS

What do these verses tell you? How do they speak into your life? What is in your life that is pulling your attention away from God?

_____

_____

_____

_____

_____

_____

_____

_____

_____

_____

_____

_____

_____

_____

_____

_____

Pig Moment 2
IT'S A LOVE THING

Following that night of revelation about my fears and release from their grip on me, I began hearing from God daily. It is as if a blockage had been removed and now the channel was wide open. There have been times in my life I sensed Him communicating direction or giving answers, but nothing that compared to what I was now experiencing. It is as if I had been deaf and then suddenly, I could hear. That may seem a bit overdramatic, but it truly was that significantly different.

The peace of God had overtaken me, and I just wanted to bask in Him every moment. I have always loved worship, but now it was reaching deeper in my spirit. I started playing music the minute I awoke each morning and right before I would go to sleep. I started being more intentional about my time. I began listening to teaching and preaching, reading books, diving into my Bible, praying more intentionally, and just immersing myself in everything I could, to keep that peace and closeness with Him.

The next Monday, I was at The Front again ready to worship and open myself up to whatever He had to show me. With each week, God was revealing Himself and like an onion, He was gently peeling off my layers. I pressed in more with each week and the Holy Spirit kept pressing into me as well. Again, I went home refreshed and walking in peace, despite the uncertainty in my life circumstances. God was just giving me peace to trust Him with my life.

A few days later, while home and reading, I heard the Holy Spirit ever-so-quietly nudge me and say,

> *"You do not understand how much We (Father, Son and Holy Spirit) love you."*

This was not an audible voice, but it may as well have been, as it was that clear in my spirit. For a moment, I was silent and a bit stunned. What? How could I not understand this? I have been walking with Christ for over 40 years. Then the Holy Spirit pushed a bit further and gently told me,

> *"You are leading a ministry called Daughters of the King and you are standing on stage telling women that their identity is in Christ, and yet, you do not believe it yourself."*

Wow . . . You could have knocked me off my feet, had I not been sitting down. I had to stop and process this new information. Could this be true? I sat there for several minutes processing this information. Then I began to speak aloud to God as though He were sitting right there with me.

> *"Ok, God. I do not know how much You love me. But I also do not know how to change that. I want to understand how You, Father, Jesus, and the Holy Spirit all love me, and how You each care for me. I am so sorry I have not seen this before now."*

I felt an overwhelming peace again. It seemed odd. Wouldn't it make more sense for me to feel shame or guilt?

The fact that I felt peace, confirmed that it was God whispering to the spirit within me. I headed to bed and slept like a baby.

The next morning as I awoke and before I even sat up in bed, I again heard a gentle whisper …..

> *"good morning child.... Last night you learned that you do not understand how much We love you. Because you do not understand Our love for you, it makes you incapable of loving us."*

Talk about having the wind taken out of your sails and being in a place of total humility before the Lord! I instantly knew it was true. I sat up with tears running down my face and again started a dialogue with Him.

> *"Oh Father, You are right! I have no idea how much You love me and as a result, I cannot possibly love You as I should. God, I have no idea, how to understand Your love or how to love You. I am willing to learn. I will not take control and try to figure this out by reflecting on it for hours and then trying to come up with a plan. I will trust You to show me Your love in ways I can understand it and I will trust You to give me a deep abiding love for You."*

Over the years, I have heard teaching about how we conceptualize God much as we do our earthly fathers. When I worked on my counseling degree, this was reinforced through psychology and counseling theories. While I knew it to be true, I thought it applied to everyone but me. I am sure some of you reading this are thinking the same thing. You understand the concept, but think you have moved beyond your past relationship with your father.

For those of you who had a very loving and God-honoring father; you have the basis for a strong relationship with our Heavenly Father. For those of us with less than perfect, or downright dysfunctional relationships with our earthly fathers, well, we have nothing of strength to draw from.

My father has been out of my life since I was seventeen years old. He was a great dad when my brother and I were young because he loved playing with us and doing all the fun stuff. However, as we got older, it was evident, we were growing up, but he was not. He did not take care of our family financially or emotionally. I thought that I understood the difference between my father's love and God's love, but I did not. I understood in theory, but applying that to my heart is an entirely different story.

All the fears God had shown me a few weeks earlier were caused by this broken relationship and not having a secure, dependable, and loving father in my life. In my teens and early twenties, I did all I could to keep people at a distance. I sabotaged every relationship with sarcasm and built walls to keep people at a distance.

At age twenty-five, I realized that my father, who was not even in my life, was controlling who I was every day. At that point, I knew I had to forgive him to move on with my life. I laid aside my hurt and anger and forgave him. It was complete, and I have not looked back. In some ways, I healed and had move on. Yet, it did not change my lack of understanding of the role of a father or being able to feel the love of a father and knowing how to receive that love.

Since I did not trust my earthly father to love and care for me, I found it difficult to trust God to love and care for me. While I do not feel anger, or hate toward my father, there are no real feelings about him and I certainly could not say I loved him. I had no idea how that was influencing my relationship with God!

I have no problem praying to God for other people, but I have never really felt comfortable praying to God for things for myself or even asking others to pray for things in my life. While typing this TODAY, God showed me that it has nothing to do with humility and everything to do with trust. I do not petition God for things in my life because I do not trust Him. This is a direct reflection of not trusting my earthly father. The question becomes, "How do I change so that I trust God?" I do not have the answer to this question yet, but God is working in my heart and spirit every day to teach me.

I am a princess not because I have a prince, but because my father is a king.

—Anonymous

REFLECTION
Understanding A Father's Love

I John 4:19 tells us that "we love Him because He first loved us." We cannot even love Him unless He first loves us. It is His love that teaches us about loving Him and others. He seeks the lost. We do not seek Him, He is not lost, mankind is.

> *There is none who understands; There is none who seeks after God. They have all turned aside; They have together become unprofitable; There is none who does good, no, not one.*
> Romans 3:11-13

Even as Christians, we often do not seek Him, but simply respond to His love extended toward us. We get caught up in the "stuff" of life and make other things a priority over seeking Him. He continually comes after us, seeks us out, leaves the 99 to find us and bring us back into the flock (Matt. 18:12-14 and Luke 15:3-7). God commands us to love Him with all our heart, soul and mind.

> *Jesus said to him, "You shall love the LORD your God with all your **heart**, with all your **soul**, and with all your **mind**. This is the first and great commandment.*
> Matthew 22: 37-38

Heart in the Greek is kardia (kar-dee'-ah) and it means inner life, intention, the affective center of our being and the capacity of moral preference. It is used over 800 times in the Bible and does not mean our physical heart.

Soul in the Greek is psuché. It means "to breathe, blow" and is rooted of the English word "psyche" (psychology). *Soul (psyche)* is defined as a person's distinct identity or individual personality; (a) the vital breath, breath of life, (b) the human soul, (c) the soul as the seat of affections and will, (d) the self, (e) a human person, an individual.

Mind in the Greek is dianoia (dee-an'-oy-ah). It means critical thinking or thorough reasoning. It includes looking at both sides of an issue to reach a meaningful conclusion

From the center of our being (heart), with His vital breath in us (soul), we reason (mind) to love God with all our emotions and will (soul). We only can love Him because He loved us. If we do not understand that He loved us, then our ability to love is obstructed. It is easy to observe in our society those that do not know His love. They are often filled with hate and anger toward others. We see it in the media and on Facebook posts.

When people use their heart, soul, or mind without God's light and power it can also be self-destructive.

Heart   Jeremiah 17:9; Proverbs 4:23

Soul   Proverbs 29:11; Galatians 5:16-24;

Ephesians 4:6; James 1:20; II Timothy 1:7

Mind   Luke 1:51; Ephesians 2:3, 4:18; Colossians 1:21

It is sad that some reject Him when His love is available for everyone at any time. He is always seeking us!

A.W. Tozer suggested the most important thing about each of us is what comes to mind when we think about God (Batterson, 2006).

> *. . . the most portentous fact about any man is not what he at a given time may say or do, but what he in his deep heart conceives God to be like."* He went on to say, a *"low view of God . . . is the cause of a hundred lesser evils"* and if you have a high view of God, you are *"relieved of ten thousand temporal problems.*
> ~ A.W. Tozer

Our view of our earthly father often transfers to our view of our Heavenly Father. When that view of our father is one of mistrust, bitterness, anger, rejection or any negative emotion, we take that feeling into our relationship with God, our Heavenly Father. We may think it is resolved, but it may be subconsciously buried deep within. If we have past issues with our earthly father, we need to spend time seeking God to be sure we have forgiven. We need to put those issues under the blood of Christ and laid them at the foot of the cross, without picking them up and walking off with them.

We need a right view of our Heavenly Father. He is loving and kind. He created us to be in fellowship with Him. He wants our time and attention. Think about how often you attempt to acquire someone's undivided attention. We even complain when we cannot obtain that from those we love.

Yet, God is always there to give us His undivided attention. He longs for one-on-one time with us and we are too busy chasing "likes" on social media or seeking out the attention of a friend or family member.

Yet, our Heavenly Father is patiently waiting for us to have a conversation with Him. He even wants us to just sit quietly in His presence. He will speak to us if we will take time to listen and seek Him. He will care for us because He is a good, good Father!

Take time to read **Psalm 23**. It tells us of the many things the Father does.

The LORD *is* my shepherd;
I shall not want.
² He makes me to lie down in green pastures;
He leads me beside the still waters.
³ He restores my soul;
He leads me in the paths of righteousness
For His name's sake.

⁴ Yea, though I walk through the valley of the shadow of death, I will fear no evil;
For You *are* with me;
Your rod and Your staff, they comfort me.

⁵ You prepare a table before me in the presence of my enemies; You anoint my head with oil; My cup runs over.
⁶ Surely goodness and mercy shall follow me
All the days of my life;
And I will dwell in the house of the LORD forever.

Verses about our Heavenly Father

I Corinthians 8:6 (ESV)
Yet for us there is one God, the Father, from whom are all things and for whom we exist, and one Lord, Jesus Christ, through whom are all things and through whom we exist.

Ephesians 4:6 (ESV)
One God and Father of all, who is over all and through all and in all.

James 1:17 (NKJV)
Every good gift and every perfect gift is from above, and comes down from the Father of lights, with whom there is no variation or shadow of turning.

Psalm 103:13 (ESV)
As a father shows compassion to his children, so the Lord shows compassion to those who fear Him.

REFLECTION QUESTIONS

Describe your relationship with your earthly father. How does that impact your relationship with God?

_____

_____

_____

_____

_____

_____

_____

_____

_____

_____

_____

_____

_____

_____

_____

Pig
Moment 3

IT BEGINS
AT THE
CROSS

Pig Moment 3
IT BEGINS AT THE CROSS

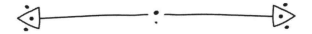

Monday was becoming my favorite day of the week. This week, the speaker at The Front was a woman named Sharon. She was so meek and yet so strong. She talked about healing in mind, spirit, soul and body. I watched her as she ministered to a woman on the front row who was crying. She continued to speak to the audience while placing her hands on this woman's head and pulling her in close. She would talk to us and then gently tell the woman that God was healing her from the emotional pain and scars. It was amazing to see the gentleness of God working on the weeping woman, while the speaker continued to share God's Word with us.

Sharon then walked us through a visualization. She asked us to close our eyes and visualize a cross. It could be on the beach, a hillside or a field or wherever we saw it. She then said to visualize ourselves at the cross. Then to turn and see Jesus standing at the cross with us. As she walked us through this process, I closed my eyes and could see nothing. I kept trying to visualize a cross and a few times I would see one for a second or two, and then it would be gone. Part of me felt frustrated, yet, the past few weeks had taught me to just wait on God and let Him work. While I could not understand why I could not see the cross, I could trust God and continue to walk in His presence.

A few days later, I had an interview for a fulltime faculty position at a local college. I had been placed in a temporary, fulltime position for a year and now had to interview for the permanent, tenured position. I had been praying and asking God for favor in the interview. God had given me peace, but that did not mean peace that I had the job. It was peace, that whatever the outcome, it would be part of His plan for my life. I did my best in the interview and then rested in God, knowing it would be several days before I would hear any news.

The next day was Good Friday and Michelle was hosting a Passover Seder meal at her home. I offered to help in the preparation, so I went early that afternoon. Michelle was the only person from The Front that I knew at this time. I was headed to her house, where there was going to be lots of people I did not know. As I mentioned earlier, social events were NOT on my list of "top 10 things" I love doing. My introverted-self would rather stay home with my dogs. My entire life I have had high anxiety in social settings, and generally just avoid them, unless I know the group of people well. However, I was so hungry for a move of God that I did not want to miss any opportunity to go deeper with Him. Cameron, my 15-year-old great nephew, and I climbed into the car and we headed to Michelle's house. He was not too excited to be going either, but his mean Aunt (that would be me), made him go. *Wheeeeeee,* here we go!

After dark, they built a bonfire and began the Seder meal in small groups. The dinner was led by a couple that spends a significant amount of time in Israel. They explained each step in the meal. There were so many direct connections to the Biblical prophecy of Christ. When we finished, the leader of each group began to wash the feet of each person in his or her group. The girl leading my group started with me. I had no idea how I would respond as she began to wash my feet. She spoke words over my life. Tears began to flow and again, such a release.

As this was happening all around the fire, the woman leading the Seder was walking in and out among the groups with a large sheer red flag/banner. It was beautiful. Once our group finished, I noticed she had removed the banner from the pole and it was being held by the four corners. It was windy that evening and it was as if God was blowing a breeze under the banner to hold it up. People were standing under it and praying. I watched for a long time and then when there was no one else under the banner, I walked over and positioned myself under it.

I closed my eyes and began to pray. I was asking God to keep peeling back the layers and to show me how to fully surrender to Him. I felt a hand on me and the woman had begun to pray over me. I cannot tell you most of what she prayed, as I was still praying. Then I heard her say, "*Jesus wants to dance with you.*" Immediately, I saw a field of green grass and a small hill. I knew I was standing there, but could not see myself. I saw a hand come out as to beckon me. I reached out and took the hand and knew it was Jesus. We began to dance. I could see us dancing across the grassy meadow toward a hill. Then we stopped and when I looked at the hill, there was a cross. For a moment, I just took it all in. Then Jesus pointed to the cross and said, "*I did that for YOU.*" At this point, the tears were streaming down my face and I felt overwhelmed by His love.

God had given me the cross I could not see a few days earlier. It was so much more powerful than it would have been on Monday night. He had made it personal for me. He was showing me His love for me. He was saying, "*I love you so much that I died for YOU. I love you so much that I kept you from seeing the cross on Monday, so we could have this time together, just You and me.*" I could have stood there forever! I had never felt as much love as I felt at that moment. He was already beginning to show me how much He loves me. He was showing me that my understanding of His love begins at the cross and with the sacrifice of His life for mine.

What we do with the cross makes the ultimate difference for each of us. His sacrifice on the cross only changes those that accept Him. The cross is the beginning of walking in a new life. We must accept what He did for us and lay ourselves down at that cross as well. The Bible tells us to be "crucified with Christ" (Galatians 2:20). We lay down our right to our life and let our will die, to be raised in new life, just as He was raised from the dead. We do not stay at the cross or we cannot be a vessel for His use. We must be raised up as a new creation in Him, resurrected in newness of life (Romans 6:4). Baptism reflects this picture perfectly. We are gently placed backward and under the water, as a sign of being buried with Him in death and raised or resurrected out of the water, to walk in newness of life.

God had once again found a unique and very individual way to show Himself. I could hardly wait to see how else He would reveal Himself and His love to me. As Cameron and I climbed into the car to head home that night, I thought…. *Wheeeeeee, Wheeeeeee* all the way home!

There were around a hundred people that came that evening. It was several days later, the Holy Spirit pointed out that I was completely comfortable! No anxiety! Wow, God really was showing up for me in life changing ways. I knew God had lifted something off me on March 27th, but I was not sure what. Now that became clear - - it was my social anxiety and it was completely gone. I had suffered with this my entire life and God had taken it in an instant, just as completely as, He healed a leper in the Bible. Not even a trace of it was left. *Wheeeeeee!*

The LORD will hear when I call to Him.
Psalm 4:3

Now this is the confidence that we
have in Him, that if we ask anything
according to His will, He hears us.
I John 5:14

For I know the thoughts that I think toward
you, says the Lord, thoughts of peace and
not of evil, to give you a future and a hope.
Jeremiah 29:11

REFLECTION
God Loves Making It Personal

God cares about the birds in the air, the grass, and the lilies, so how much more does He care about us, His creation (Matthew 6:25-30)? God used a burning bush to gain Moses's attention in Exodus 3. He cared so much about communicating with this *one man* and created something special. God cared about the nation of Israel and wanted to use Moses to free them from bondage (Exodus 14). He created a miracle at the Red Sea to *save a nation*. God again used a miracle when He had Balaam's donkey talk to Balaam to keep him from walking into danger (Numbers 22:1-39). God demonstrated that He cares about *the direction* we are headed in this miracle. He multiplied the widow's oil to provide for her and her son (II Kings 4) and multiplied the loaves and fishes (Mark 6:30-44) to show that He cares about *our daily provision*.

God does things to chase us down and get our attention. He performs miracles in all our lives to show us His love for us. I think back to the circumstances that surrounded several of the teenagers that came into my home through foster care. In several instances, there were mountains in front of us that seemed insurmountable in our strength. At times, we were going up against the foster care system, birth parents, and sometimes just the difficult circumstances that were part of these teenager's lives.

God did miracle after miracle in rescuing these teens and making a way for them to become a part of my home. Yet, from day-to-day, I forget the past miracles. It has been ten years ago now, and I let the miracles slip my mind when I face a new mountain. I would guess, I am not alone and some of you have done the same. God performed miracles in your life and at the time, you were aware and thankful. Yet, time passes and the next detour or mountain comes along and you have forgotten about the Red Sea miracles in your life.

That is why journaling can be so important for us. Journal what we are going through and how God brings us through it. Then when the next difficulty arrives, we can look back and be encouraged as to God's faithfulness. He is faithful and will take care of us.

God knew you in your mother's womb before the foundation of the earth and He has a plan for your life.

Psalm 139:13 *For You formed my inward parts; You covered me in my mother's womb.*

Jeremiah 1:5 *Before I formed you in the womb I knew you; Before you were born I sanctified you; I ordained you a prophet to the nations.*

These verses can be applied directly to YOU. He sees YOU individually. He knows YOUR joy and pain, YOUR desires and disappointments. He hears YOU when YOU pray.

He will have encounters with YOU that are just as personal as my dance with Jesus that night on the grassy field. He wants to love on YOU and show YOU His love in many ways. Sometimes, we just need to be still and quiet enough to hear Him. Let Him lavish His love on YOU!

REFLECTION QUESTIONS

Think back to times God showed you His love in a personal and specific way. Write about it here.

_____

_____

_____

_____

_____

_____

_____

_____

_____

_____

_____

_____

_____

_____

_____

_____

_____

REFLECTION QUESTIONS

What do these specific situations tell you about His love for you?

_____

_____

_____

_____

_____

_____

_____

_____

_____

_____

_____

_____

_____

_____

_____

_____

_____

_____

Pig
Moment 4

SO MUCH
MORE

Pig Moment 4
SO MUCH MORE

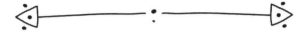

Yay, it is Monday again and the day right after Easter. Once again, the worship brings me to a place of a vertical relationship with Abba Father. I have been intently praying for favor for the job interview I had the week before. A part of me wanted to reason things out, listing all the reasons why this job was the right fit for me. Certainly, God had opened the door, so why would he close it now. I pushed those thoughts from my mind and focused on God's presence. Whatever He has planned for me, is where I will learn to rest.

As the worship continued, I heard the Holy Spirit whisper, "So much more." My attention is immediately heightened. "What does that mean?", I asked. Again, I hear, "I have so much more for you." *"Ok, Holy Spirit, I heard you . . . . does that mean I will get the job or does it mean you have something else, something more for me?"*, I replied. No answer came, but I was suddenly filled with peace that God had all this in His hands and that I had prayed for favor in the interview and that is what He was giving me.

Two days later, I received a call from the college telling me that I was not selected for the position. At that moment, I felt disappointment and sadness. This meant in just a few weeks I would have no fulltime job and no benefits. That day was crazy busy and I did not have time to even process or to stop and pray. My schedule was non-stop until nine that night. As I walked into the ladies Bible study that evening, God was settling my heart. I shared with the ladies what had happened over the last week and how God had been speaking to me in ways I have never experienced. I told them about God saying to me "so much more" and then getting the word that I did not get the job. I had to trust what I knew: GOD IS FAITHFUL. He never leaves us and He wants only what it best for us. So, that meant that God had, in fact, given me favor. I had not received a job offer because of His favor. He has something else in mind and I just need to trust Him to lead me.

What I did not realize at that time is that favor is not for us! God gives us favor for others. The same is true of anointing. If God gives us favor or anointing, it is to work through us to influence the lives of others for His kingdom. Favor and anointing are to bring glory to God, not to us. So, I did not get the job because God was showing favor on my life, so I could do other things for His kingdom. He did not want me at a job that might take away from His plan for my life. His plan is always better than our plan.

Later that week, I sat down with the Dean of Academics, who is also a Christ follower, and told Him that God must be leading me to something else or to do more ministry. It was great to have that conversation with no resentment or anger over not getting the job. Even though he knew I was a Christian, he seemed surprised by my positive response to the news. God had closed one door, which meant He was going to open another door.

The next week, despite not getting the job and not knowing how God would provide for us financially, I began to hear the Holy Spirit talk to me about giving. At this point, it would be natural to say, *"Are you kidding God, I do not know where my income will be coming from a month from now and you are going to talk to me about giving?"* Yet, here we were, me and God, having this conversation Okay, so maybe it was not much of a conversation. It was mostly the Holy Spirit nudging me and telling me that He was about to change my giving significantly.

I am now weeks away from no income and He is telling me where to give money, when it seems like I should be saving every possible dime. Based on the past six weeks of the condensed learning, I did not even debate it and just surrendered. I went to my computer and gave to the three ministries He impressed upon me. Two weeks later, I did the same thing. I had no hesitation as I believe that God can best supply my needs when I am faithful to surrender to His will.

So, if that is not crazy enough, the next step He asked me to take, really put my cognitive abilities in question. The college position had not been offered to me, but two days later, I was asked to send my resume to a local high school to teach English. I spent six hours doing all the paperwork and submitting it. I told my pastor's wife and good friend, Jennifer, about this possibility. She used to be a school teacher and I thought her insights would be helpful. While talking, I also told her that I was sensing in my spirit that this might not be where God wanted me and He might ask me to turn down the job. Tears were running down my cheeks as we spoke. She said she hoped God would simply close the door if it were not meant to be and that she could not imagine walking away from an offer with no other job in hand.

The next week, the high school called me for an interview. It was now mid-May and one week after my job ended. Over the past several days, I had convinced myself to just walk down this path, after all, God must have opened this door, right? The interview went well on that Friday and I should have left happy and excited about this opportunity. Instead, I felt unsettled all weekend. The peace I had been walking in was now turning to anxiousness. I felt deep in my spirit that the job was not where God was leading, but kept trying to convince myself that I would walk through this door and let God close it if He chose.

On Monday, I spent some time with two friends and expressed a bit of my uneasiness. Not really going into the full detail of what I felt God was telling me because I am not sure I wanted to hear it myself, and speaking it would have been admitting it. I bet many of you reading this can relate to times in your lives when you heard God speaking a message that you absolutely wanted to rebuke. I know I am not alone in this tale. However, my friend Bonnie, true to herself, spoke wisdom and truth in a very loving way. She said she did not know how I would be able to do ministry, as God was calling me to, and work this forty-plus hour a week job. Zing. . . . I felt the sting in my heart. Truth had been spoken and it immediately rang true in my spirit.

So Much More

It was Monday, so that meant off to The Front! At this point, I can hardly wait for Monday to roll around each week. As I walked in that evening, I began to pray, "Father, I need to know your will concerning this job. I want you to tell me tonight, beyond any shadow of doubt, if you want me to walk away from this." During worship, He gave me the answer. It went something like this. . . .

> *"My daughter, I am so glad you have come to a*
> *point of surrender so I can do great things in your*
> *life. You already know the answer... it lies in the*
> *peace. I gave you my peace weeks ago and the only*
> *time you stepped outside of that peace was during*
> *the interview for this job. I have the best possible*
> *plan for you, . . . walk in peace and I will take care*
> *of your needs."*

My response was simple . . . *"Ok, Lord."*

I texted Bonnie immediately. I needed to tell someone to confirm what I had just told God, so I would not back out of my surrender. God created us to work together, to grow together and to support each other on this journey. Sometimes that comes in the form of accountability and this was one of those times. I also sent message to the DK Community team and my Bible study group.

As soon as I woke the next morning, I sent an email to the assistant principal who had interviewed me. I thanked her for the interview and told her I had to remove myself from the pool of candidates as I was "called to another position." She responded within minutes, telling me it was "their loss" and she hoped I would be happy in my new position. I emailed her back telling her it was not a "job", but that I felt called to put all my efforts into ministry. I had no idea how she would respond to that information. She was probably thinking, "Is this girl crazy to walk away from a fulltime teaching position with benefits?" The answer would be, "Yes". Apparently, I am either hearing directly from God, or I am crazy. She sent me one more email telling me if I changed my mind in the future, to contact her, as they would love to have my skills on their team.

Mixed emotions came. Wow, I would have received the job offer. . . that makes me feel good. Or does it? satan was trying his best to work on my mind over the next few hours. "What if you are wrong?" "What if you are wrong about what God is saying?" "What if you do not have the money to pay your bills in a month?" I prayed, I put on worship music, I prayed some more. Several of the women from our DK team had sent me encouraging messages about stepping out in faith. God was sending reinforcement through them. Within just a few hours, satan had given up and my peace was intact.

All the answers of how God would provide were unclear then, but I was one hundred percent confident that I had followed what the Holy Spirit told me. I had to rest in the One who is Faithful and True! My Rock, my Shield, and my Refuge. He is the only one who can give peace. Everything else is a very distant second to His peace. *Wheeeeeee!*

> *Now may the God of hope fill you with all joy*
> *and peace in believing, that you may abound*
> *in hope by the power of the Holy Spirit.* Romans 15:13

REFLECTION
Sometimes FAVOR means "NO"

No is a difficult word to for most of us to accept. There are not many circumstances that we consider "*no*" a good word. Research shows that just seeing the flash of the word, "*no*" for one second, will cause a release of dozens of stress-producing hormones and neurotransmitters. It can cause anxiety and depression. So, what happens when the "*no*" comes from God?

The best way to frame this question, is in the context of a parent-child relationship. Parents say "*no*" to their child for many different reasons. Sometimes it is to keep the child safe.... "No, do not touch the hot stove." Sometimes it is to teach values and character .... "No, do not take something that does not belong to you." Sometimes it just not the right timing .... "No, you cannot eat the cake before dinner." Sometimes it is because the parent has more experience and knowledge about the future outcome .... "No, you cannot go to that party." While parents make mistakes too, they still have more years' experience in understanding natural consequences for actions. They can better predict outcomes and their job is to teach values and keep the child safe.

God, our Father, has all knowledge and He never makes a mistake. He created us and only wants what is best for us. He can see the difference between what is good and what is better. He sees into the future and knows the long-term ramifications of each decision. And most importantly, He loves us more than our earthly parents and wants nothing more than to see us prosper, and live in peace and joy.

I wonder if Joseph was wondering why God had given him a dream and then allowed his brothers to throw him in a pit and sell him into slavery (Genesis 37). It would stand to reason that Joseph would have been praying and asking God to get him out of that terrible situation. Apparently, God said, *"No!"* We can look at Joseph's entire story and see many times God said, *"No"* to fixing his situation. He said, *"No"* to clearing his name in front of Potiphar (Genesis 39). God said, *"No"* to rescuing him from prison (Genesis 30-40). God allowed the butler to forget him once he was back in Pharaoh's house. Things looked bleak for Joseph. Nothing seemed to be going Joseph's way, yet he kept earning favor with the people around him. God gave him favor because of his character and because that favor would help others.

God also knew more about his future than Joseph could possibly see. He was positioning Joseph for a much larger task of saving a nation during seven years of famine (Genesis 41). God raised him to a position that was second in the kingdom, but it took a lot of "no's" and thirteen years to get there. How many of us would have as much faith as Joseph? He did what was right despite being treated horribly by his brothers, the false accusations of Potiphar's wife, and being forgotten after interpreting dreams in jail. I must be honest and say, I am not sure how I would hold up under those same circumstances. How about you?

Joseph was honorable through it all. He kept his faith in the God of Abraham, Isaac, and Jacob. We do not see any record of him crying out to God and saying, *"This is not fair"* or *"Why me."* He took each *"no"* in stride and did not lose faith. The next time you are feeling sorry for yourself, read Genesis 37-41.

The best part of the story is that through it all, God gave Joseph favor with those around him. No matter where Joseph landed, the Lord was with him, he had favor, and God prospered him.

Gen 39: 3-4, 21-23

3 And *his master [Potiphar] saw that the LORD was with him and that the LORD made all he did to prosper in his hand. So Joseph found favor in his sight, and served him.*

21 But *the LORD was with Joseph and showed him mercy, and He gave him favor in the sight of the keeper of the prison. And the keeper of the prison committed to Joseph's hand all the prisoners who were in the prison; whatever they did there, it was his doing. The keeper of the prison did not look into anything that was under Joseph's authority, because the LORD was with him; and whatever he did, the LORD made it prosper.*

God's plan was so much bigger than Joseph could have imagined. If he had not been in jail, he would not have met the butler and been brought before Pharaoh to interpret the dream. If he had not interpreted the dream, then a nation would not have been saved from the famine. The bigger the call of God on our lives, the bigger the challenges we may walk through to prepare us.

REFLECTION QUESTIONS

What No(s) has God given you?

_____

_____

_____

_____

_____

_____

_____

_____

_____

_____

_____

_____

_____

_____

_____

_____

_____

_____

REFLECTION QUESTIONS

How has this chapter helped you to reframe those into God's divine knowledge of what is best for you?

_____

_____

_____

_____

_____

_____

_____

_____

_____

_____

_____

_____

_____

_____

_____

Pig
Moment 5

The Hem
of His
Garment

Pig Moment 5
The Hem of His Garment

It was Thursday, June 1st and I woke up with pain in my right arm. My health benefits ended on May 31st. Let me back up to give a bit of history ....

I had spinal surgery four years ago. I had pain in my right arm on-and-off for about two years. The doctor had told me it was from all my computer work. Then one day I woke up in excruciating pain and it was constant for three weeks. I tried the chiropractor, acupuncture, massage, the family doctor, etc. I ended up in the ER with Morphine directly into my vein and was still in pain. After four hours, I left the ER and went home still in pain.

The next day, I went back to my massage therapist. He took one look at me and refused to lay a hand on me. He told me to go my doctor and demand a MRI. I took his advice and had the MRI two days later. The doctor called me the next day and referred me to a neurologist. As soon as the neurologist looked at my MRI results, they called and asked me to come in the next day. He told me I had three crushed disks in my neck and the broken pieces were floating around and hitting a nerve that affected my right arm. The surgeon told me he had no idea how I was tolerating the pain. I had no idea either, except GOD! He told me he could fix the problem and I could live pain free.

Tears rain down my face at the thought of no pain. Two days later, I was in surgery. I awoke from the surgery and did not even have the sore throat he had told me I would have from the surgery process. *Wheeeeeee!*

While I would not want to repeat this experience for anything, God taught me something important through the process. I had been living in so much pain that it was almost impossible to believe the doctor when he told me he could do the surgery and I would be pain free. I had two choices. I could step out in faith and trust the doctor's word and have the surgery or I could choose not to believe that it was possible to be out of pain. I could have said to myself, *"What if it doesn't work and then I am worse off after the surgery?" "What if the doctor messes up?"* There was a list of "what if's" I could have chosen. Instead, I chose to go for it! Wow, am I glad I did. Even the recovery was almost pain free. I have titanium in my neck, but NO pain!

Through my surgery, God showed me that He offers forgiveness and a new life. Some of us step out and trust Him and others stay in unbelief. Maybe you have said to yourself, *"What if God isn't who He says He is? What if God cannot fix this situation? What if this person leaves me if I stand for God? What if God doesn't provide for me?"* The enemy will give you lots of "what if's" to try to keep you from surrender. Just like I had to trust the doctor to do the surgery to remove the floating pieces causing my pain, you need to trust God to remove the sin and unwillingness to surrender that is causing your pain.

I was standing on a stage at a women's conference just three weeks after my surgery and had that story to share of

God's forgiveness and love and that we just need to step out in faith and believe. God took a situation that was painful (literally) and used it for His good. He gave me favor so I could share my story and influence others.

Ok, back to June. I woke up with the same pain in my arm. I was trying to convince myself I was imagining it, but it was very real. I went off to a conference that night hoping it would stop. Nope! And it did not stop the next day or the next. Four days later, I was trying to figure out what I would do. The last surgery cost $55,000. Yes, you read that right. However, now I had no insurance and I just started on a Christian sharing program, for my insurance needs the very day the pain returned. I had not told anyone about the pain. I knew if I told my mom, she would drive me crazy until I went to the doctor. The same would have been true for my best friend, Deb.

On Monday, Bonnie called me. I told her and she suggested I get prayer at The Front that evening. In my head I said, *"Yea, that is not happening."* However, I was in so much pain that day, that I decided, IF I possibly saw an opening, I might tell Michelle while we are in the prayer room. As it turned out, they did not have prayer that evening because they were having a mission meeting. I was sitting with an hour to wait before the service began. Judy, a lady on our Front team, came in and sat down on the other side of the room. A few minutes later, I saw her approaching me. She looked me square in the eye and said, *"Where is the pain in your body?"* I was a bit taken back, but I told her and explained about my past surgery. She asked if she could pray for me.

She began to pray and asked God to remove the pain from my arm and to heal any issues in my neck. It only took her a minute or two and then she asked me my pain level. I told her it was the same. She prayed again and they looked at me and said, "God is healing you" and walked off. I stood there hoping the pain would be gone.

You must understand that I come from a conservative Baptist, background and there is not much talk about healing. I fully believed God was capable and that He still healed people. I had heard of people being healed, but had never seen it or experienced it. I decided to believe that God, not only could heal, but that He would heal. I began praying myself and asking God to heal me. The pain began to subside. Thirty minutes later it was almost completely gone and 15 minutes into worship – it was gone! *Wheeeeeee*!!! I went over and told Judy the pain was gone. I was somewhat in shock. Believing God can and even believing He will, is different from believing He would heal ME.

The Holy Spirit brought to mind the story of the woman who had a twelve-year blood related disease (Mark 5:24-34). She reached out and touched the hem of His garment and was healed (according to the Greek, it was fringe of His prayer shawl). I sensed the Holy Spirit was telling me to cling to that passage.

For the next two weeks, when I would get a tinge of pain in my arm, I would reach out with my right hand as though I were grabbing Jesus's garment. I would hold it tight and say, "*I cannot touch you, Jesus, and not be completely healed. I am touching you, so I am claiming Your healing power over me.*" I also began to pray that God would strengthen my neck and make it strong again. I had a stiff neck the next several days and believe that is exactly what He was doing. After about two weeks, all momentary tinges of pain were completely gone.

I have heard about survivor's guilt that occurs when one person lives and another dies. The person who survived feels guilt. I had a few moments of *"Why me God? I see people suffering with cancer and horrible diseases, why did you choose to heal me?"* The answer that came was simple as God spoke to my heart…… *"You my child, needed to see Me in a new way. You needed a miracle in your life to step out and trust Me in a path I have for you."* From that point forward, I quit questioning and simply rested in gratitude for what He had done for me. *Wheeeeeee!* The Father showed His love for me again and in a very personal way.

We cannot understand the mind of God. He tells us His thoughts are not our thoughts and His ways are not our ways (Isaiah 55: 8-9). Yet, we try to take our finite brains, which He created, and figure out what He is doing. We spend time trying to figure out why He heals one person and not another. God is sovereign and we need to stop questioning His ways. He does not owe us an explanation. I cannot explain why He healed me that night and has not healed my best friend of Lupus. I can continue to petition Him on her behalf, and trust that He knows what He is doing at all times. I certainly cannot say the same is true for me, and I would guess you cannot say that either.

REFLECTION

He Is Still the God of Miracles

As we walk through things in our lives, it always comes down to an issue of belief. We find out in the difficult times what we really believe and in whom we place our trust. We all put our faith in something or someone. The question is, "what?" or "who?" I was presented with several choices over these past few months to determine where I would place my trust. Would I place it in a job? Could I place my trust in God for healing? I certainly could not understand my circumstances, but I could choose to have trust and faith in the one who is FAITHFUL.

"Now faith is the substance of things hoped for, the evidence of things not seen." Faith comes first, understanding second. *"Through faith we understand that the worlds were framed by the word of God, so that things which are seen were not made of things which do appear"* (Hebrews 11:1, 3).

Faith comes out of rest and surrender, not out of striving and determination. How often have you tried to work out the problem before taking it to God in prayer? How often, have you been exhausted from striving? For me, it is too often to count.

One of my favorite preachers is Bill Johnson from Bethel Church. His messages are deep and they stretch me to see God more rightly. Most of what he says is quotable…. as demonstrated on my Facebook page! Johnson made this statement in one of his messages, *"All our encounters are to help us be made into the image of God.*" Wow! If I could just remember that when I am going through something and complaining. We often go around with a, "It is all about me" mentality and that is not how God sees it. He wants to mold us into something much more beautiful than our current state. And it would be fine with me if He shaves off a few unwanted pounds for me in the process of molding me ☺. He is the potter and we are the clay. When we remember, we are clay, which is soft and able to be easily molded, He can mold us into any form He chooses. When we think, we are large and in charge, we are rigid and unable to be molded.

The word which came to Jeremiah from the LORD, saying: Arise and go down to the potter's house, and there I will cause you to hear My words." Then I went down to the potter's house, and there he was, making something at the wheel. And the vessel that he made of clay was marred in the hand of the potter; so he made it again into another vessel, as it seemed good to the potter to make. Then the word of the LORD came to me, saying: "O house of Israel, can I not do with you as this potter? says the LORD. "Look, as the clay is in the potter's hand, so are you in My hand, O house of Israel!   Jeremiah 18:1-6

Woe to him who strives with his Maker! Let the potsherd strive with the potsherds of the earth! Shall the clay say to him who forms it, 'What are you making?' Or shall your handiwork say, 'He has no hands'?   Isaiah 45:9

Woe to those who seek deep to hide their counsel far from the LORD, And their works are in the dark; They say, "Who sees us?" and, "Who knows us?" Surely you have things turned around! Shall the potter be esteemed as the clay; For shall the thing made say of him who made it, "He did not make me?" Or shall the thing formed say of him who formed it, "He has no understanding?"   Isaiah 29:15-16

But indeed, O man, who are you to reply against God? Will the thing formed say to him who formed it, "Why have you made me like this?"   Romans 9:20

Part of this season for me, and maybe for you too, is allowing God to change me and to form me into something new. With each change He makes in me, it affects my view of Him. He is showing me Himself in so many new ways. Some of the ways He shows Himself to us is through miracles. God uses miracles to anchor our affections to a world we cannot see (Bill Johnson). He is giving us an anchor to have faith and trust in Him and it sets our affections on things above (Colossians 3:2). One miracle in our life should lead us to trust Him for the next and so on.

If we understand all that God is doing in our lives, then we have reduced God to our understanding (Bill Johnson). I certainly want a God bigger than my understanding. How about you? If we want Him to do a deep work in us, our walk will be in mystery much of the time, because it is a walk of faith, trust, and abandonment. I want to walk in a new place of the miraculous. I want to see God for who He is and not who my theology has made Him out to be.

God has been stretching me and showing me more of Himself. He wants to be known by us. He wants us to see Him for who He is and to allow Him to mold us into His image. He is still the God of miracles and His power has not dwindled since New Testament times. I believe He performs miracles in all believers' lives. Sometimes we just do not recognize them or remember the ones He has done for us.

REFLECTION QUESTIONS

How has God shown Himself to you? Has He performed miracles in your life that you have too soon forgotten?

_____

_____

_____

_____

_____

_____

_____

_____

_____

_____

_____

_____

_____

_____

_____

_____

Pig
Moment 6

The
Rear-View
Mirror

Pig Moment 6
The Rear-View Mirror

Over the next few months, God continued to work to form and mold me into something new. This did not mean things were going well around me. My great nephew, Cameron, was struggling in many areas and had so much anger that it affected every waking moment of his day and most of mine. His parents live in another state and he had been in Florida for three years. Things came to a head during the summer and I bought a plane ticket for him to return to his parents. I told him that he needed to resolve his anger with his parents and if he could not do that, then he would need to stay there. I had to set boundaries to not be the target of his anger.

Our past will bubble up inside us, come back to haunt us, and taunt us, if not addressed. All his past was bubbling up and spilling over to everyone around him. He needed to stop looking in the rearview mirror, stop running from his past, and stop denying there was a problem. It was time to face things head on. I knew it would be very difficult for him to do, but I could no longer allow the destructive behavior. Something had to give before I fed him to the alligators…. LOL… I am just kidding!

Things were very quiet and calm here for the three months he was gone, but things were not calm there. I heard about problem after problem. After much prayer, I insisted he be put on a plane back to Florida, even though I knew I would have to deal with his rage. I had legal custody, so they had to send him back here at my request. He was not happy at all about coming back, as he did as he pleased there, with no rules. My home functions much differently, with structure, common courtesy and respect. He came back in late October and was even more angry than before.

In late November, I felt the Holy Spirit telling me to do a forty-day time of intercession for him and not to expect any changes during that time. I bought a new journal and began the process of daily seeking God for this sixteen-year-old's life. There was no change and in some ways, it was worse.

While dealing will all his past issues, God started dealing with mine. In December, I had made a trip to see friends in Ohio and my daughter, Vennessa, in Kentucky. I was in Hamilton, Ohio with my friend, Sue Thurston. She is an amazing woman of God, who leads ministry endeavors all over the world. After we had lunch, I had planned to travel on to Washington Court House, Ohio to see my friend, Candy Pfeifer. As I pulled out of the restaurant driveway, I felt a strong sense that I needed to go to Miamisburg, where I was raised. I pulled out my phone and called my sister-in-law, Tricia, to let her know I was coming.

It is only about a 45-minute drive and I had worship music on, just singing and enjoying my trip. I had taken some back roads into town and as I crossed into Miamisburg, I was overcome with emotion and tears were streaming down my face. They seemed to come from nowhere. Based on the experiences of the last year, I immediately asked God.... *"What is this about?"* I heard the Holy Spirit say, *"We are healing your past.*" My first thought was, "*What does that even mean?*" I sensed I needed to drive by the three houses I had lived in growing up. I pulled into the park behind the one of the houses. I prayed, "*God, what do you want me to do?*" His response was, "*Nothing! I have done the work in you, so you need to do nothing.*" *Wheeeeeee!* When God does a work, it is complete and there is no need to stress about it or continue thinking about it. I went on about my day. Headed to the Hamburger Wagon for the best hamburgers ever, visited with family, and then headed to Washington Court House. I spend a few days with Candy and then drove back to Florida.

The forty days of prayer for Cameron ended in January and three days later, there was a huge blow up with him at youth group. I received a phone call and started praying as I drove toward church. The situation was very tense, but when he climbed into the car to head home, something changed. There was a significant shift in his demeanor. He began being more respectful, he started doing his school work and was just much more pleasant. He started really plugging in at church, rather than just attending because I made him. He was helping the youth pastor one day a week, running sound on Wednesday nights, and recording fun videos with some of the interns. WOW. What a shift. Another *Wheeeeeee* moment!

How cool is it that God heals us both physically and emotionally? He had healed me physically and He is beginning to do some work in Cameron, to heal him emotionally. Little did I know, He was just beginning the emotional healing for me.

I have never been a person that looks back. I live more in the future than even in the present. Even a glance in the rear-view mirror is infrequent for me. God was about to teach me that it is sometimes necessary to look back if you have not dealt with the issues. Ignoring them, does not make them go away. The glance in the rear-view mirror is only healthy when you have first faced your past head on. I ignored the past and thought it would go away. It did not! If I never look in the rear-view mirror, I am bound to back up and run over something or someone. Or I might be dragging some of the past behind me and I would not even know. For me, the rear-view mirror was running from, as opposed to glancing back, to keep me on track.

Just as I did not look back at all, some of you are looking in the rear-view mirror for too long. It should be to see what is around you and gauge where you are. However, if you keep looking back, you will run into something or run over someone. Just as we must address our past, we cannot camp out there. We must step out of the past and into the present. We cannot move into the future without being in the present.

How we handle situations and stress determines our view. We are either looking forward or looking backward. If we avoid the situation, we keep moving without addressing the issues. If we wallow in the past, we cannot move into our future. Which direction are you looking, forward or backward?

REFLECTION
Getting Past Your Past

Each of us handle difficulties and hurts differently. When we feel hurt, or encounter difficult circumstances, we experience STRESS. Stress can be defined as a person's adaptive response to a stimulus that places excessive psychological or physical demands on that person. There are said to be six different styles to handle stress (Patterson, Grenny, McMillan, and Switzler, 2011). These fall into two categories: Silence Patterns and Violence Patterns. Silence patterns include things like avoiding potential problems, withholding information, and verbal games. Violence patterns involve attempts to control, convince or compel others to see things your way. All these are harmful, so do not assume that silence is better than violence. All of them are indicators that we have not moved past our past.

The **SILENCE STYLES**:

Masking. This includes understating or selectively showing our true opinions. Sarcasm, sugarcoating, and couching are some of the more popular forms. If you are like me, you are saying… "What is couching?" Couching is to express indirectly or obscurely, to hide or conceal.

Avoiding. This involves steering completely away from sensitive subjects. We talk, but without addressing the real issues. It is like avoiding the elephant in the room.

Withdrawing. This means withdrawing from a situation or conversation altogether. We either exit the conversation or exit the room.

The **VIOLENCE STYLES**:

Controlling. This includes coercing others to your way of thinking. It is done through either forcing your views on others or dominating the conversation. Methods include cutting others off, overstating facts, speaking in absolutes, changing subjects, or using directive questions to control the conversation. Expressions like, "You never do it right."

Labeling. This is labeling a person or ideas, so we can dismiss them under a general stereotype or category. Expressions like, "Christians are all hypocrites."

Attacking. This is when you move from winning the argument, to making the person suffer. Tactics include belittling and threatening the person. Expressions like, "Are you stupid?" "You are too skinny to be pretty."

** Violence Styles are classic "bullying" techniques.

If you find yourself doing any of the silence or violence styles, you may need to look at your past. There are undoubtedly unresolved issues from your past that you are bringing to your present and that will affect your future.

Growing up I was a master at Masking! Even into my early 20's, sarcasm was my favorite tool. I was afraid to let anyone get too close, so I used sarcasm to keep people at a distance. I used this tool much less as I got older. In 2007, I took parenting classes for foster care and I truly came to understand that sarcasm is hurtful and inappropriate. I cannot say I never use it, but as soon as I do, I want to take it back.

Sarcasm, by definition, is "a sharp, bitter, or cutting expression or remark; a bitter taunt or gibe." You notice the definition says nothing about "just kidding" someone. I now believe there is never a right time or way to use sarcasm. It is hurtful by its very nature.

There is progress as I do not use Masking any more. However, in a stressful situation where I feel rejected or threatened, I will run to Withdrawing. Now, there are times to withdraw for a period, while both parties take a time-out. Yet, it should not be an ongoing way to manage stress and conflict. It is an indication that something is unresolved deeper inside me or you that we need to look at.

My great nephew on the other hand, uses all three of the violence styles. He was sitting with me as I wrote this today and saw the three styles and I asked him if he saw himself in any of them. He read them and smiled. That was admission! He and I had a brief and not too deep conversation about our styles. Too much or too deep and he would have bolted out of the room for something much more fun. ☺

So, the question becomes, what areas of our past are still haunting us? Are you spending more time looking in the rear-view mirror than you are looking ahead? If you continually look back, you are bound to crash into something. How do we face our past and then move past it in a healthy way? Pray and ask the Holy Spirit to reveal any areas in your past that may be negatively affecting your present. Take some time to pray and then journal on the next page what you feel God is revealing to you.

REFLECTION QUESTIONS

Do you spend too much time looking in the rear-view mirror at your past? What do you see in your past?

_____

_____

_____

_____

_____

_____

_____

_____

_____

_____

_____

_____

_____

_____

_____

_____

_____

REFLECTION QUESTIONS

What things from your past are affecting your present?

_____

_____

_____

_____

_____

_____

_____

_____

_____

_____

_____

_____

_____

_____

_____

_____

_____

_____

Pig Moment 7
Music, Music, Music

It is now the end of January 2018, and I generally go on a cruise with my best friend and her family. The cruise is with a group of Southern Gospel artists, many of whom I have come to know over the past fifteen years. Now, if you are saying, "What is Southern Gospel?", ask your grandma. Bill Gaither is probably a name your grandma will remember. There are many groups in this genre of Christian music and the lyrics are powerful, just as they are in Contemporary Christian music. I happen to have grown up on Southern Gospel. I started listening to Contemporary Christian music only ten years ago. I love both styles and feel sad for those of you who are in a habit of only listening to one or the other. Ok, enough on that soapbox!

This cruise is a great time of refreshing for me. I get to hear great singing and preaching for five days and hang out with my friends. My best friend, Deb Talley, who I have mentioned before, has been traveling and singing since she was nineteen. We have known each other for forty-plus years. (I am not sure how that is even possible since I am only 29 and she is only 35 - - that is what we will admit to anyway). While I lived in Tennessee, I occasionally traveled with The Talleys (Deb, Roger, and Lauren) over a weekend to help at their product table and just to hang out. During this time, I met many of the other artists in this field. Yeah, so I am kind of famous….. not!

On this cruise, I had coffee with Sheri Easter, a sweet southern belle. As she and I talked, I shared with her some of what had been happening with Cameron. Sheri and her husband Jeff, were coming to Bradenton right after the cruise and we decided to meet up for lunch and for me to bring Cameron to meet them. The plan was to engage Cameron by asking him to help bring equipment into the arena. Cameron is a hard worker and when we see the Talleys he is always the "roadie" for the night. He loads and unloads, and just loves helping.

I told Cameron and he was not happy about having lunch with "my friends" but I told him Jeff needed his help. We met them and Cameron liked Jeff immediately. Jeff is just the kind of person that everyone loves. After lunch, they insisted he ride with them on the tour bus to the arena. I met them there and by the time I got there, Jeff had him up on stage schlepping instruments and equipment. Jeff was introducing him to all the artists. I ran into Karen Peck (another artist) and she said in her southern voice, "I met your nephew, Cameron. He is so sweet."

Cameron went from the boy who did not want to even be there, to the life of the party. He helped set up and then, we headed home for a brief time. I planned to go back for the concerts that night. Cameron had told me earlier in the day, he was not going to hear them sing. Several of the artists had asked him if he was coming back, so when it came time for me to leave, he was in the car. We would listen to the artists and go backstage and talk to them. At the end of the night, they were hugging on him and telling him how much they enjoyed meeting him. Are you kidding me! I have known these people for several years, what am I, chopped liver? I teased him about stealing my friends. I could not have set up the evening and planned it the way it turned out. God took over! These incredible artists, gave of themselves and loved on him.

A month later, The Talleys were in our area for two days. Deb gave Cameron a shirt that says, "Roadie." He has a major crush on Lauren and will kill me for putting that in this book. While at their product table, he saw a brochure for an event in Myrtle Beach. He was insistent that we would go in April. It took some finagling, but I found a way to make it happen. This is the first time he has shown interest in anything I like and in this type of music, so I was ready to move heaven and earth to make it happen.

We traveled to Myrtle Beach for five days of Gospel music. Cameron had met several of the groups in February, so he went around talking to them like he has known them forever. He made me take him out to get some dress shirts and shoes so he would look nice. Really, a sixteen-year-old who wants to look nice for adults…. Has this boy lost his mind? He was determined to leave with one of the groups and become the product guy. I heard him trying to sell Bill Shivers (from Brian Free and Assurance) on why they needed a product guy. It cracked me up. He is a bit shy when he does not know people, but he was in the auditorium by himself, listening to all the groups and loving it. Deb said to me, *"Would you have ever thought this could be possible?"* *"Heck NO"*, was my response.

For those of you who are not familiar with Southern Gospel music, let me tell you who this sixteen-year-old likes, so you can look them up on Apple Music.

- The Talleys
- Karen Peck and New River
- Brian Free and Assurance
- Jeff and Sheri Easter
- The Hoppers
- The Whisnants

Cameron had his picture taken with Jeff Easter, Karen Peck, Bill Shivers, Deb Talley and Lauren Talley. When we look at the pictures, we laugh and say that these artists, wanted their picture with him. It was a fun week and for the first time, we shared in something we both really enjoyed. *Wheeeeeee*, all the way back to Florida.

Thank you to all these amazing artists that made a young man feel special. It is a testament of your walk with the Lord. I love and appreciate all of you!

I wondered if it would wear off when we returned home, but it has not. He talks about the next time we will see them and how he is going to travel with a Southern Gospel group. I am fine with anything that points him toward God and making good choices! God is faithful! Following His direction to pray for forty days, changed everything. Once I moved out of the way, God worked in miraculous ways. *Wheeeeeee*! Here we go on a new journey.

REFLECTION

God Performs the Best Harmony

Too often I have tried to figure things out and make things happen in my life. I bet I am not alone in this, and many of you reading this have done the same. I am the logical person who believes I can solve any problem that comes my way. As soon as I hear of a problem, I go into problem-solving mode. I can quickly see three or four possible solutions to the problem. While there is nothing inordinately wrong with this, I can step out and try to fix something without even consulting God. I grow frustrated with those who cannot see how simple the problem is to solve, if they would just do it my way. Yep, I am that person, or at least I used to be.

In this season of my life, God is trying to break me of this habit. I am learning to take a deep breath, count to ten, pray, stand on my head, or anything else to cause me to slow down before I jump ahead of God. I may have a good plan, but if I can just sit still long enough and listen to hear the heart of God, He has a better plan!

I could have tried to work out all the details to try to ensure that Cameron had a good evening or met all the right people. I could have tried to place all the instruments in the right place at the right time. Yet, God did it effortlessly. He brought each person into harmony with His plan for Cameron. He leaves the ninety-nine for the one, and that is what He was doing for Cameron.

We can see examples of this in the Bible, too. Abraham and Sarah tried to help God with the son of promise (Genesis 16). God made the promise and He is certainly capable of delivering on it. Peter even thought he had a better plan for Jesus (Matthew 16). Peter rebuked Jesus' plan… can you imagine? We might think that is just crazy, but we do the same thing in our own lives. At least Peter heard Jesus' plan. Often, we are too busy or in too much of a hurry to even hear Him.

We want the best for our children, parents, spouses, friends, etc. Yet sometimes, our zeal and impatience get in God's way. Sometimes He cannot even work in someone's life because we have put ourselves between that person and God. He needs us out of the way, so He can work. Getting out of the way is hard. It feels like we are sitting by and watching the situation and not doing anything. We do not have to sit idly by, we can pray. Prayer is one of the most powerful tools He has given us. It allows us to sit back and watch God work miracles in the lives of those around us.

God is the master musician and He will make beautiful harmony if we just let Him work through each instrument. The instrument has no beauty without the musician to play it. He can orchestrate things for our best when we allow Him to do so. Let Him use you as an instrument to flow through into perfect harmony. Then you too, can say *Wheeeeeee* and bask in His presence.

REFLECTION QUESTIONS

Can you recall times when you tried to orchestrate every event in someone's life? What was the result? Have you seen God work when you let Him?

Pig
Moment 8

Not
Wrecked,
Totaled

Pig Moment 8
Not Wrecked, Totaled

Eight is the number of new beginnings, so how appropriate for this to be Pig Moment 8. With each new beginning, something must come to an end. So, let's begin to talk about the endings that started new beginnings.

Let me back up and describe what I do to make a living. I am a college instructor (on campus and online) for three different universities. These are part-time, so the work varies from semester to semester. I do some Pastoral/Christian counseling as God sends women or teens that need help. I was also part-time staff at a local church. In addition to my paid work, I lead DK Community, and volunteer on the ministry team for The Front. No …. I am not busy at all!

The day after Cameron and I arrived in Myrtle Beach for the Southern Gospel event, I received a call from the church, asking me to resign. They felt "I was not following the _____ denomination" closely enough. I could not disagree. I do not follow a denomination, I follow Christ and Biblical principles. For that, I will not apologize. I felt hurt and disappointed. It was also going to immediately affect my income.

We returned from our trip and the next Thursday I was in a serious car accident. It was my fault. I looked in my rear-view mirror for a second and when I looked forward ….

brake lights! Crash! Remember that we talked about what happens when you look in the rear-view mirror. My airbags had imploded and my car was filled with smoke. It took me a minute or two to determine, it was a powder from the airbags. I attempted to put the car in park but the gear shift would not move. This meant I could not turn the car off either. I tried to open my door but it would not open. Tried the passenger door, it would not budge. I rolled the windows down to clear the smoke so I could see and assess the situation. After four or five minutes, I was able to crawl out one of the back doors.

I immediately went to the woman whose car I hit and asked if she was okay. She turned and began to verbally blast me. I was a bit shocked. The bumper on her SUV was damaged, but my Corolla was no match for an SUV. The front of my car was crashed in, which is why I could not open the doors. I was concerned about her well-being, but she was not concerned about mine. I totally understand, I hit her, but really? She had been out of her car and on her cell phone for several minutes and I had just crawled out the back of my car.

As I walked back to my car, a sheriff had stopped and asked if he could help. He just happened to be driving by on the same road. He and another man were able to get my car to the side street and get it turned off. He told me the FL Highway Patrol was on the way and warned me to stay away from the other driver. He had heard her ranting and said it would be best if I not even talk to her. The next two hours consisted of sitting at the scene of the accident until my car could get towed and I could get picked up. My service advisor from the Honda dealership came and picked me up. She even called and arranged the tow truck for me. Thanks Tammy!

Everyone else had left the scene and I was alone waiting on the tow truck. I kept repeating over-and-over again, Thank you, Jesus! The car I hit was either stopped or close to it and I was going around thirty-five miles an hour. I do not know how many of you have been in a wreck, but it happens so fast and yet it seems to be in slow motion.

When my car hit the back-end of the SUV, my body never moved in my seat. I mean, it never went forward and backward as one might expect. The front and side airbags deployed and never touched me. It was as if angels were holding my body and head in place. I had no mark from the seat belt, no mark from the airbag, because it never touched me and I was not sore at all. The next morning, I half expected to wake up to soreness, but there was NONE. *Wheeeeeee*! My only mark was on my left pinky. I must have hit it on the side door panel. It had a small bruise about the size of a pea and was only sore if you touched it.

I have already told you about my spinal surgery, so being worried about my neck would be natural. I had no pain but had a CT Scan to be sure everything was okay. They said all the titanium plates and bolts were still in place and everything looked great! Thank you, Jesus! *Wheeeeeee*!

So, while my body was good, the wreck was trauma like I had never experienced. I tend to just shrug things off and move on but I was unable to just shrug this off. The unkind words of the woman in the SUV, kept replaying in my mind. I was feeling anxiety at a high degree. Yet, I was going to approach this like everything else.... Just get on with the next thing.

Friday, I woke and felt a bit shaken. I had planned to attend a dinner for the House of Prayer, but I did not want to drive! A young couple from The Front picked me up. Thanks Sophie and Dinu! I thought I would be fine, but I was a nervous wreck all night. I was so happy to get home that evening. I was having flashbacks of the crash all through the day and dreaming it at night. I woke up and said to satan, *"NO, you will not torment me with this."*

On Saturday, I felt like I needed to go to King's Station for the Saturday night service. I was not afraid to drive, but was overly cautious. As soon as I arrived there, I was overcome with anxiety. I just felt I needed to be at home. It must have been visible, even though I thought I was masking it. After the service, Gary from Galatians 6:2 and Joy, the OMC Prayer Link Coordinator, each asked me if I was okay. Joy and I sat down to talk. I told her about the wreck and how angels had held me in place and I had not been hurt.

She began to pray over me. In her prayer, she thanked God for the angels protecting me. She abruptly stopped praying and looked at me. She said that the wreck was prophetic over my life. She said that God is holding me in place or position just as angels did during the wreck. Then, she said that my car was totaled and that God had totaled my life and everything from this point forward would be new. Keep in mind, this is two days after the accident and the insurance company had not even seen the car yet, so I had no idea if they would deem it totaled. She then began to speak encouraging words over me. I drove home that night and still had all the anxiety, but I also had hope. What she had spoken over me, resonated in my spirit.

I have heard many people say, "I'm wrecked for God" or "God wrecked me." I had said to a group a few months ago that God had "totaled me" while on a city outreach. At the time, I did not even think, that is just what came out. After giving it some thought, when a car is wrecked it seldom, if ever, drives the same no matter how good the mechanic. I do not want a wrecked car. I would rather it be totaled so I can drive a new one. The same is true of my life. God needed to total it and then make it new. I do not want to be wrecked and walk around with internal bumps and bruises. Joy's word to me had completely aligned with what God was already telling me. Her word was right on, and the insurance company did determine my car to be totaled just a few days later.

Sunday morning, I drove Cameron to Woodland for church and decided to stay there for service, since I was no longer on staff at the other church. I had the same experience as the day before. I was fine driving there, but as soon as I arrived, I felt panic and could not wait to get home. The next day was Monday, so off to The Front. As worship was playing, I was seeking God. I asked Him to take the anxiety and the flashbacks. When I left that night, they were gone. Not one since - thank you, Jesus! *Wheeeeeee!*

A few days later, I received a call, inquiring about a student from one of my college classes. I forwarded all the communication between myself and the student. As an instructor/teacher, you will have students who love you and others who do not like you or what you do or how you do it. I generally let this roll off me, but this time, I let it sink deep into my soul. I could not shake it. I even said to God, *"Ok, enough. How much more can I take right now?"* The Holy Spirit quickly reminded me that Jesus was criticized and He was sinless. Why would I be so puffed up to think I am better than that? WORD!

On top of these circumstances, I also had no confirmed classes for the summer term. No classes, means no income. Registrations are down at most of the universities and that affects those of us that teach as part-time instructors. It is now mid-May and I am feeling like I have been hit back-to-back with things. I was walking around with such a feeling of heaviness. While the anxiety had lifted, I now found myself in depression for the first time in my life. I tried all the things I thought would work to feel better. I listened to worship music, preaching, read my Bible, but nothing changed. Remember, I am the one with three to four solutions to each problem, and yet, nothing I tried worked. I felt like I was walking around in a cloud of depression and worry.

This continued for a few weeks. Bonnie had called me twice trying to talk me out of the deep place I was in and would pray with me. She asked if it was helping and I said, *"No, but I appreciate you trying."* I knew all the scriptures about casting my care on God and that He had promised to take care of me, but it did not comfort me one bit. I sat in the chair in my bedroom for over four hours that day, listening to worship music and preaching. I was determined not to get up until I heard from God. Bonnie called during this time and told me I needed to be FULLY PERSUADED of God's power and might. Zing…. Right to my heart.

That did not lift the heaviness, but it gave me something to pray into. Hope had appeared as a small light at the end of the tunnel. Picking up my Bible, I began to dig in. From that simple statement from Bonnie, came my personal decree. This decree did not instantly solve all my fears, worry and depression, but had given me something to read every day and to hold onto. It gives me hope in the One who is all I need. Some of the darkness lifted that day, but not all of it.

Joy had invited me to lunch a few days later. As we sat and ate, she looked across the table at me and told me that when she looked at me, she wanted to cry. I do not consider that a compliment, and I thought, "Oh geeezz, is it that obvious?" She said she saw such "heaviness" on me. I did not have to wonder how she knew that. The Holy Spirit has a way of revealing things to us as we connect with people. He loves us so much that He chases us down to show us His love through others. The Holy Spirit will speak to others as a way of reaching us.

As we ate lunch, I shared with Joy my current struggle. We then moved to the living room with coffee and just started talking about the goodness of God and all He has done in our lives. In an instant, the heaviness lifted and was gone. No one prayed over me, no one rebuked the spirit of depression. We simply were focused on the GOODNESS of the FATHER. I did not say anything as Joy was sharing at that moment. When she finished, she looked at me and said, *"What just happened? Your entire countenance has changed."* I told her the heaviness and depression were gone! *Wheeeeeee!*

Throughout these difficulties, Bonnie reminded me that not all bad things that happen are from the enemy. Sometimes, God is shifting us through our circumstances. That was some of the best advice I have heard in my entire Christian walk. Too often, we just start rebuking the enemy and do not look inside ourselves. I started to ponder that and asked God to search my heart. God began to show me many things in my own heart.

Little did I know what He was about to show me......

But You, O LORD, are a shield for me,
My glory and the One who lifts up my head.
I cried to the LORD with my voice,
And He heard me from His holy hill.

Psalms 3: 3- 4

MY PERSONAL DECREE

I Declare and Decree . . . .

I am FULLY PERSUADED that you, Father, have a plan for my life (Jeremiah 29:11).

I am FULLY PERSUADED that you, Father, are the lifter of my head (Psalms 3:3-6).

I am FULLY PERSUADED that Abba, my Father is and will take care of me and my needs (Malachi 3:10 and Luke 6:38).

I am FULLY PERSUADED that you, my God, have a reputation for breaking into impossible situations and reversing the affect (Luke 1:37).

I am FULLY PERSUADED that the Spirit of the Lord is upon me and I will be changed for His glory (I Samuel 10:6 and Isaiah 59:21).

II Tim 1:12 *"For the which cause I also suffer these things: nevertheless, I am not ashamed: for I know whom I have believed, and am persuaded that He is able to keep that which I have committed unto Him against that day."*

Rom 8:38-39 *"For I am persuaded that neither death nor life, nor angels nor principalities nor powers, nor things present nor things to come, [39] nor height nor depth, nor any other created thing, shall be able to separate us from the love of God which is in Christ Jesus our Lord."*

Luke 1:38
"Let it be unto me according to thy word."

REFLECTION

Endings Create New Beginnings

Endings are difficult. Whether it is the end of a good time or a difficult one. It could be the end to our favorite movie or spending time with our best friend. We do not want those times to end. An ending may occur because a relationship is over or you were laid-off from a job. Each ending creates a new day and new opportunities. When we leave a visit with our best friend, we may be sad, but tomorrow is a new day and we now have those memories from the time we shared together. The memories add to the strength of the relationship. When a relationship that is not working ends, it is because the relationship itself was more painful than ending it. When we lose a job, it may leave uncertainties for the future, but often, we find a job that is even better.

When I realized, I would have no work, thus no income that summer, I was almost in panic mode. I knew the Bible told me God would take care of me…. But what if He didn't? I was allowing the enemy to keep whispering negative thoughts and was consumed by them. Bill Johnson once said, "Whenever we give in to negative emotions, it is like we are saying to God, 'I'll be back in a minute' and we side with satan."

I did not start the day off as I should, and left my mind wide open to attack. I concluded that I could fix this problem and could just go get a job. I am employable, after all. I had no sooner processed that thought and I heard the Holy Spirit say, "*Yes, you can 'fix' this and I will still love you and bless you because you will not be walking in disobedience or sin. OR you can do this Our way, and wait on Us and start walking in a new place. You can start walking in faith and miracles."* Really, Lord? You are going to put it like that?

Deciding to follow God did not make all my emotions die at that moment and I still walked through several days of struggle. However, God comes through and gives us peace and joy in the midst of the circumstances. Loss of a job and no summer classes also meant time to do something else. I began to pray about what new beginnings God had purposed for me. What did He want me to be doing? He has pulled my work, a church, my car, so He must have a BIG plan.

For ten years, I have felt called to write books. In a matter of weeks, four different women, spoke words over my life. Three of these women, did not even know my name. They each confirmed what God has already placed in my heart; that I was to write. Time had not permitted and I felt like I was in a waiting pattern. Two months ago, God said, *"Get on it girl."* Yes, He talks in slang from time-to-time. I finished the book I started ten years ago, in only three weeks. *Detours - That Become Life's Path* was released in August 2018 on Amazon and Kindle. The time off, made it possible for me to focus. It seemed clear God had very intentionally orchestrated this time off. There is perfect harmony when He leads the orchestra.

Last summer, I started journaling about these "pig moments" and knew God intended it to be a book. I had some notes on the first two chapters, but had not touched it in nine months. As soon as I finished *Detours*, I started this book. With nothing else to pull my attention, I have worked on it faithfully every day this week and God has given me a chapter a day. What seemed like a curse (no work), has been a blessing. This book was written in eight days. *Wheeeeeee*! That is God!

Cameron was still attending Woodland because he was connected to the youth group there. Now, I had to figure out what God wanted me to do concerning a church home. The weekend we came back from the trip, I went with him back to Woodland. It was great to be there and see all my old friends. God settled my heart that morning, that it was not where He wanted me for this next season.

Since I was involved at The Front and King's Station, joining another church would be splitting my ministry time even further. Miracles had occurred in my life this year through the freedom I have experienced in these places. It was clear, my place of ministry for this season was not going to be a local church. Instead, God was calling me to pour my time, talent and treasures into different areas for this season. A new beginning!

As for my car.... I had just lost a new car to flooding in September. In Florida, we have big rain storms that result in floods. Yep, it was me, floating down the road in my car full of water. I only had that car for nine months. The car I wrecked in April, I only had for six months. In my defense, the car before those, I had for eight years. After all this car stuff, I would just rather have a chauffeur, and never drive again. Like that is going to happen... not.

Cameron is sixteen and has his driving permit. He will get his license in next January (if I don't feed him to the alligators before that ☺). He and I sat down and talked about cars. Now, this is not a discussion you want to have with a sixteen-year-old boy. They think a fast car is better than food and if you have ever had a teenage boy, you understand just how big a deal that is. He had saved money from his summer job, last year and I took it from him and put it in an account he could not access, so he would have it toward a car. In his words, "I stole his money." I proposed that we get a car that would be his once he obtained his license. He could make the down-payment and I would make the payments while I drove it. He is to get another job and start saving to pay it off.

It was a miracle, but we agreed on a car. They accepted his down-payment amount (yeah, the money I stole). As he drove the car off the lot that day, I asked him how he felt about me "stealing his money, now?" He laughed and thanked me for not giving it to him in all his whining. This car has given him a new focus and is teaching him responsibility. He cleans it almost every day and is driving me crazy about it, but I am glad to see him so excited and learning about responsibility. A new beginning!

The moral to this story is that often endings look bleak and are painful. Yet in God's kingdom, they are simply new beginnings. He makes everything new. He will make beauty from ashes and turn mourning to joy. He is an awesome Father! *Wheeeeeee* for new beginnings.

REFLECTION QUESTIONS

What endings have come in your life?

_____

_____

_____

_____

_____

_____

_____

_____

_____

_____

_____

_____

_____

_____

_____

_____

_____

_____

_____

_____

REFLECTION QUESTIONS

What were the new beginnings that followed?
How did God take care of the things you
worried about?

_____

_____

_____

_____

_____

_____

_____

_____

_____

_____

_____

_____

_____

_____

_____

_____

_____

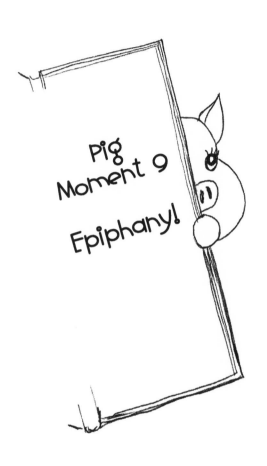

Pig
Moment 9

Epiphany!

Pig Moment 9
Epiphany!

If you have walked with God for any length of time, you know that His timing is perfect. He brings us alongside others in a time of need, and He places others in our lives to come alongside us. He allows us to walk through things and later, uses it to help someone going through a similar situation. God has done this many times in my life and I am sure He has in yours as well.

While completing the final two chapters of my first book, *Detours: That Become Life's Path*, God gave me an epiphany. Each chapter in *Detours*, is a true story of someone's life and then I took one element from each story and discussed it from both psychological and Biblical perspectives. One of these stories was about rejection. As I began researching rejection. God started speaking to me in ways I did not expect. While I was looking at this topic in the context of another person's story, He began to touch my heart and show me unresolved issues in my own life. I was in the midst of the heaviness and depression and God revealed that at the core of the issue was rejection. Losing the job, rejection. Having an accident that was my fault and being verbally assaulted by the woman, rejection. Student complaint, rejection. Epiphany!

According to Merriam-Webster, an epiphany is "a sudden manifestation or perception of the essential nature or meaning of something; an intuitive grasp of reality." Some might say that suddenly, the "light comes on" and we see things clearly. You flip the switch and suddenly you have light. To place that in the Christian context, darkness must leave when the light comes on. It would make sense that you see things clearly and can put circumstances in perspective when the light comes on and the darkness flees. As you are walking around in a dark unfamiliar place, you feel your way and try to determine, where you are and what is in front of you. It is much the same when we are in a place we have never been before emotionally or when we are in a dark place where there is little or no light of hope.

The word *rejection* used in reference to my life was an epiphany. Suddenly, the light had been shed on a hidden place. This was not something I would have thought was an issue in my life. I am sure some of you are like me, and you just get up from a situation and move on, possibly with little or no emotion. What I did not realize was that the rejection was still there. I just learned to bury and ignore it.

Over three or four months, I had several dreams about a man I dated years ago. The dreams are not the same, but the story line was. At the end, I am rejected and someone else is chosen over me. One Sunday night, I had this dream. You know how you try to force yourself to wake up, so it will stop? I was trying to force myself to wake up. I began questioning God as to why I am dreaming about someone from over twenty-five years ago. The Holy Spirit gently whispers, "You are having these dreams because you are

still carrying the rejection from the relationship."
Epiphany!

The following Tuesday, I met my friend, Jennifer, for lunch and shared with her about the dream and what God had told me about carrying the rejection. She stated how surprised she was that I had been struggling at all over some of the recent events in my life. She said it seemed like I handled things so well and she would never have guessed I had been struggling. I had learned to *mask* so well that I could teach that class. I thought Jennifer knew my story, but she did not. I shared my history with her and as I shared details, she pointed out that the events were rejection upon rejection. It was eye opening for me to see my life through someone else's eyes. All the way back to my parents' divorce at age ten and my dad leaving me with my stepmom at seventeen. I was not harboring any anger or resentment, but I was carrying rejection.

Over the next several days, I prayed over this new insight. I asked the Holy Spirit to show me how to move beyond the rejection of the past, so it would not be in my present and thus affecting my future. I want God to be able to use me as a vessel for His kingdom and I felt this was a stumbling block to walking where He may lead. I was getting no specific answer from the Lord, but continued to seek Him each day for wisdom.

On Saturday evening, I decided to go to King's Station for the service. It consists of worship and a then speaker from our region, who could be sharing on a variety of regional issues. During worship, I went to the back of the room, laid face-down on the ground and prayed. No answers came and

I returned to my seat anticipating the speaker would start soon. The speaker for this week was Joy, the prayer link coordinator for the OMC. She said she felt like healing was happening during the worship time and asked the man leading worship to continue. I was still seated, but began to pray again. I was not in an emotional state at all, yet tears began to stream down my face and hit the floor. I knew the Holy Spirit was working in me at that moment. He began to show me times of rejection from my childhood to the present. As He began showing me, I said, "*Father, what do you want me to do with this information?*" The Holy Spirit told me to verbally confess each instance and give each one to Him. As He began to show me, I confessed it and turned it over to Him. I had no idea what all this meant, but knew to follow His instructions in surrender.

Sunday, I shared with Joy what God had done in me. It was important for her to know that she was hearing from the Lord, when she stepped out to change the plan for the evening. I am still not sure how this will manifest in my life from day-to-day, but believe God will show me as I walk it out. I had no idea what happened, when He took my social anxiety until days later and I have had NONE since March 27, 2017. I am FULLY PERSUSADED He has now done a work in me to remove the rejection.

Monday night came, and off to The Front. I usually stay up front during worship and then sit on the second row. We have a small coffee shop by the door and I was working it that evening. In the door walked Sam, and behind him, Miriam. They were as stunned to see me as I was to see them. Miriam is one of the teenagers that came into my home through foster care. She came to live with me in July 2007 at age fifteen, along with her 11-year-old sister, Jazz. She moved out on her own when she was nineteen. She lives in Orlando and I do not get to see her very often. Her brother, Sam, lived with us for one year until he turned eighteen.

Miriam and had not spoken to me for two years and it cut deep. A year and half ago, right before Christmas, I received a text from her apologizing and telling me how thankful she was for all I did to help her and her siblings. We spent two hours texting and talking and our relationship had been restored. However, I still do not get to see her often and miss her so much. While our relationship had been mended, there were still issues with her birth mother and other family members. They did not want her to see me. Now there they were, standing before me.

We hugged and exchanged the *"What are you doing here"* phrases. Sam's wife and children were there as well, and so was their birth mother. Both the parents had been addicts and had spent time in jail, which is how I ended up blessed to have them in my home. I went over to say hello to her birth mom and see how she was doing. She lives in New York but was in for a visit. I looked her square in the eye and said, *"Are you clean?"* She said, *"Yes"* and that she had accepted Jesus and has been walking with Him for the past year.

Wow, God had done it again! He showed up in a way only He could do. I had experienced rejection from several of the eighteen teenagers I had taken into my home. I adopted seven of the teens and became permanent guardian of

Miriam and Jazz. Many of these teens did and said very hurtful things as they turned eighteen. Many of them chased after birth parents and turned their backs on me. I had given all I had to them to keep them safe, loved them and taught them about the One who would stay with and love them forever, Jesus. The pain was real and ran deep through my heart as they moved out and some chose to not talk to or see me. REJECTION!

I found my way back to the coffee shop area. A few minutes later, here came their birth mother. She embraced me so hard and so long that I could barely breathe. She kept saying, *"Thank you for taking in my kids, thank you for keeping them safe, thank you for introducing them to Jesus."* Can you imagine? What a moment of restoration for everyone. God was showing me, He could take care of the rejection, now that I had given it to Him. That night, I went home with peace from all that happened. *Wheeeeeee!*

In the middle of the night I awoke from a dream. This dream was about my grandmother. I have dreamed about her from time-to-time since her death in 2001. In the dreams, she has come back to life, but I cannot seem to find her or connect with her. I always awake frustrated and sad. This night, I dreamed again that she was alive and so was my grandfather. I was in their house in Kansas and we were all sitting in the family room. My grandmother was very disappointed in my decision to date the man I mentioned earlier. In the dream with my grandmother, I am apologizing for my bad decision. She never speaks, but a smile comes over her face. It is the first time, I could see her in my dream and while there were no words, I felt her forgiveness and approval. *Wheeeeeee*! God has just done it again! He is removing the rejection.

This journey the Father has for me is not yet complete. I do not have the total *Wheeeeeee* ending, but I am sure it is in my future. God has a way of gently showing us the areas in our life that are keeping us from being more like Him.

As mentioned in the beginning of this section, God brings us alongside others who need our help and are experiencing a similar struggle. It is no coincidence that Cameron's main struggle is based in rejection. I buried mine and acted like nothing happened (avoidance). He buries his and denies he has it, but it comes out in anger and rage. The same deep-seated issue and two different ways of dealing with it. God has much to teach us both. He has me walking through this, so I can also help Cameron. God's love is so amazing in how He orchestrates our lives into beautiful harmony.

These journeys we travel are often difficult and we can either walk them in faith or fear. I CHOOSE FAITH. My God is able! The next few steps are unsure, but I know if I trust Him, He will continue to mold and form me to His image. I have experienced Him taking my social anxiety, my physical pain, my depression and heaviness. That gives me confidence and hope that He will lead me through the steps of releasing the spirit of rejection over my life. *Wheeeeeee*! I am looking forward to what the Father has next for me.

Behold what manner of love the Father has bestowed on us, that we should be called children of God! Therefore, the world does not know us, because it did not know Him.
John 3:1

REFLECTION

Accepted, Not Rejected

When my adopted kids would get mad at me, they would say, *"You're not my real mom."* To which I would reply, *"I know I am not your birth mom, and I CHOSE you to be my child."* While they were rejecting me, I was showing them I accepted them. How much greater is a love by choice then by default. I am not saying I loved my kids more than a mom who gives birth to her child, yet the sacrifice is different when it is by choice.

God tells us we are accepted as His adopted children. He willingly gave the sacrifice of His Son so we could be His sons and daughters. He loves us more than we can imagine. Even when we mess up, He still loves us. His love is truly unconditional and that is hard to understand because we have never had anyone love us that way. He accepts us when all others have turned their backs on us. He loves us even when we make bad choices. His mercies are new every morning (Lamentations 3:22-23).

Augustine once said, *"God loves each of us as if there were only one of us."* It is difficult to conceive that He would have sacrificed His Son if we were the only person alive. It is difficult to understand why He would leave the ninety-nine for the one (Matthew 18:12 and Luke 15:4). It is difficult to understand how He can know the number of hairs on our head (Luke 12:7 and Matthew 10:30). How could He have known me in my mother's womb and already had a plan for my life? He told Jeremiah, *"Before I formed you in the womb, I knew you ... and ordained you a prophet to nations*" (Jeremiah 1:5). How can God care that much about one person? His ways are not our ways and His thoughts are not our thoughts. What do we think about most of the time …. ourselves. We do not spend all our time thinking about Him. Yet, He thinks about us all the time! *Wheeeeeee!*

Take some time to read the verses below and let them sink into your spirit, mind, and soul.

The LORD your God is in your midst,
a mighty one who will save; he will rejoice over you
with gladness; he will quiet you by his love; he will
exult over you with loud singing.
Zephaniah 3:17

For I know the thoughts that I think toward you,
says the LORD, thoughts of peace and not of evil,
to give you a future and a hope.
Jeremiah 29:11

Having predestined us to adoption as sons
by Jesus Christ to Himself, according
to the good pleasure of His will.
Ephesians 1:5

But God shows his love for us in that
while we were still sinners,
Christ died for us.
Romans 5:8

REFLECTION QUESTIONS

Write down any other verses God has given you to remind you of His unconditional love for YOU.

_____

_____

_____

_____

_____

_____

_____

_____

_____

_____

_____

_____

_____

_____

_____

_____

_____

Epiphany!

REFLECTION QUESTIONS

Write any epiphanies God has given YOU.

_____

_____

_____

_____

_____

_____

_____

_____

_____

_____

_____

_____

_____

_____

_____

_____

_____

Pig
Moment 10

He is
Faithful

The
Chapter
for
Parents!

Pig Moment 10
He is Faithful
The Chapter for Parents!

The last two months had been a struggle in our home. Since our May trip to Ohio, Cameron has been angry and difficult again. As mentioned in Pig Moment 6, Cameron's default is to use a violence style in dealing with stress. God has shown me the root is rejection in his life, but knowledge does not change the situation. I was hoping that by making the trip, it would settle his heart when we returned. It did not. Instead, it stirred up old feelings and wounds. From the moment we climbed into the car for the trip home, there was unrest. Thankfully, he had not reverted to square one, but had certainly gone backward from the shift made in his life in January.

Feeling frustrated and angry that I was once again dealing with his anger, I began to pray. I prayed in his room and played the audio Bible when he was not here. I anointed everything I could with oil and basked it in prayer. Things seemed to be getting worse, not better. We know from scripture that the enemy often fights harder when you begin to follow and obey Christ. I heard Jesse Duplantis say, "Increased favor means increased opposition" and we were living that out.

If you are a parent, you have at one or more times, experienced people who think they should tell you how to parent. Everyone has an opinion about what you should do as a parent, whether they have had children or not. Some people were telling me to "take authority" and command the spirits to leave and that if I did this, the spirits could not re-enter the house. Well, I have news for you, that is NOT what was happening. Those negative spirits would come right back in, because he was choosing to carry them.

Our friends are well meaning in their advice, but we need to listen to our heavenly Father, rather than people. He was telling me to continue to pray and trust for the next level of breakthrough. Things rarely come as quickly as we would like. I began to pray once again for a shift in Cameron's heart and breakthrough. I began to pray for his heart to be softened and for light in his life and for light to be physically manifest in his room. He likes to sit in the dark and work on his computer, watch TV or play Xbox. The darkness was engulfing him and light needed overtake the darkness.

Cameron has a special relationship with the middle school pastor, Sammy. Even before he lived here, he would come each summer for a few weeks and attend youth camp. He has bonded with Sammy and respects and admires him. He feels like he grew up in this youth group even though it was only a few weeks each summer before moving here. He has a young man, Evan, who is mentoring him as well. These two men have greatly impacted Cameron's life. Due to these relationships, Cameron volunteered to work the middle school camp in June.

The first few days of camp, one of the boys had been bragging about getting wasted and other things. During one of the night services, he got rocked by God. When I picked up Cameron that evening, he relayed the story to me. Just in him telling me the story, I could see it had an impact on him and he was talking in ways he does not normally talk. *Wheeeeeee*! He was using Christian terminology that he normally avoids. So, on one hand, this kid is getting it and on the other, he was still raging at home and with me. This indicates there was still much inner work to be done.

The following week was Vacation Bible School (VBS) and he volunteered for that too (because Sammy asked him). He loves working with kids and is very patient with them. I have repeatedly told Cameron that he is gifted with kids and music and that God might call him to be a youth pastor or to lead worship. Just working with the kids makes Cameron happy.

Two weeks later, in July, is the high school youth camp. For the first several days, they sleep at the church, perform outreach in the community and do fun things. Then, they drive to Miami to work with a church there. This meant two suitcases, one for the first few days at the church and one to take to Miami. Wednesday evening, I went to Woodland to pick up the first suitcase and bring it home. As the teens came out of the evening service, Cameron's face was all red and I could tell he had been crying. He walked straight over and hugged me. This was a miracle! *Wheeeeeee.* In the three years he has been here, he has only hugged me about three times. As we walked to get the suitcase, all the boys were very quiet.

As I drove home, I wondered what had happened in the service that evening. The next morning, Cameron called, asking me if I could come by the church. My first thought was that he was in trouble, as last year he had been asked to leave camp due to his behavior. I asked what he needed, and he said he needed to tell me what God had done in his life the night before. *Wheeeeeee!* Praise the Lord…. the shift was beginning.

I drove to Woodland and sat down with him and he began telling me that ever since the middle school camp when he saw the change in his friend, that it had been on his mind. He said he wanted to go deeper with God and wanted to get baptized again to show his commitment. *Wheeeeeee!* They were going to baptize five of the teens before leaving for Miami. I stayed and watch the baptisms with tears rolling down my face. His mentor Evan, assisted in the baptism. He spoke about the changes he has seen in Cameron this past year. *Wheeeeeee!*

So, it would seem we would stop here. So much has happened. Miracle after miracle! Not "luck" like the world might view it, but miracles performed by God. Yet, with all this happening, my heart was still uneasy. School is not a topic you want to bring up in any way, shape or form with Cameron. He hates school and it causes so much stress in our home. It is now two weeks from the start of school with NO plan. Cameron has repeatedly said he would "never go to college" and "as soon as I am 18, I am dropping out of school and moving out." As you can imagine, and maybe have even experienced, this is not a fun time. Ughhh.

It was in the middle of the semester, when Cameron came back to FL and he did not want to go to school. His mom was not making him go in Ohio and so a battle ensued to get him back into school. The outcome was that we placed him in the Florida Virtual School online. This was NOT what I wanted. It meant he was home all the time. I told him if he chose to do it, that I would get him tutors if he needed help, but that I could not be the one to help him.

I work more than fulltime with my three teaching positions and even when I am home, I am teaching online. I am NOT a homeschool mom! I work and my work is teaching, so I do not want to do that when I am off work. He also would ask for help, but then would just argue. He would tell me the assignment was stupid, his teacher is incompetent and he was not going to do it. I was exhausted from the battles this past year and said, "NO WAY" to Florida Virtual (FLVS) for this year.

Because he came back in the middle of the semester, he started school November 1st. This put him behind, so he finished his year's work the middle of July. He had not wanted to talk about next year and if I even tried to bring it up..... World War III. I called his mentor and asked him to come over to discuss school with Cameron, so I had a buffer and a witness. Cameron said he would not talk about it if Evan came over. I was now frustrated beyond my capacity. On Monday, he told me he will go to the local technical school for the Auto Collision program. I am trying to work out details of what that looks like and how he does his school classes at the local high school. I still have unanswered questions and details to work out before the next week when classes start. I dropped him at youth meeting on Wednesday night. I sat down to chill a bit and turned on the TV, trying desperately to not think about all of it for a little while. I had no peace and my spirit was stirred. I turned off the TV and began to pray.

I called out to my Father and reminded Him that I am His daughter and Cameron is His son. I reminded Him that He promised to take care of us and that this school issue was more than I could bear. As I am praying, my phone rang. I looked over and it was Cameron calling (during youth service). I answered the call assuming he wanted to ask to go somewhere after youth service. He started telling me that a girl had spoken in the service that night about what to do after high school. She felt God was calling her to do ministry and had decided to go to a college for ministry. He asked if we could talk when he came home about him doing a dual enrollment ministry program under Southeastern University.

Before you think my line to God is something different than yours, I can assure you it is not. I have never had God answer a prayer so quickly. It was not that He answered this prayer that quickly; it was all the prayers that had been sent up before this day and time. If you are a parent, keep praying. Do not give up... He will answer.

Cameron came home with his mentor, Evan. Yep, the one he did not want involved in the discussion just days earlier. The three of us sat down to talk about this possibility. Evan asked him why he wanted to do this ministry program. Great question! I am so happy when someone else is involved and asks the hard questions. Cameron said that I have told him repeatedly over the last three years that God has a plan for him and he would be a good youth pastor. WOW... he heard me and remembered it. So, when he says I never encourage him, he knows that is not true. Hope that encourages you parents! There is hope that they do hear us.

We discussed the difference between college classes and high school, expected behavior, what he would have to do for high school classes, etc. I told him I would look in to the details and follow-up the next morning, but not to be disappointed if we could not get him in for the fall start date. We did the online application that evening and I started sending emails and making calls the next day. I prayed and asked God to open the doors wide if this was the plan for Cameron.

By late afternoon, we had received a call back from the Southeastern University. They said, he could attend and to pick four classes for the year. WHAT? Seriously, how many of you parents know how long it normally takes to get this stuff done? Nothing about going to college is easy and the steps are generally long and cumbersome.

Cameron will take four classes for high school through FLVS online and then take one eight-week college class at a time. Perfect. His first college class will be Old Testament! *Wheeeeeee*! Seriously, I could not hope for more than this. His other three will be English Comp I, English Comp II, and College Math. He will also get to take Guitar at least one semester.

Cameron does not understand the entire "credit" thing, so I tried to explain how he earns credit for high school and college with the college classes. Not sure he will fully understand until he starts. He also cannot understand how he can do an eight-week class and that be equivalent to one year of high school work. After the first class, I think he will be even more excited. Cameron is brilliant, but tries very hard to hide it. His IQ is higher than average and he has the mental capacity to do this. Now I just have to pray that God will give him the necessary motivation to do it.

Cameron generally does well around adults, but not teachers. He has an overall lack of respect for authority, which is what he learned through his upbringing. I am hopeful that being in college classes will teach him new attitudes and behaviors. There will not be any kids acting out for attention in a college class. I believe this will teach him to drop the attention seeking behaviors he has relied on up to now.

During this same week, a friend of Cameron's came over. This boy only had his license for about three months, and I had not been allowing Cameron to go in the car with him. I had a rule with all the kids that they could not ride with any of their friends until he or she had their actual license (not driving permit) for one full year. I sat them down and talked about what it would look like for Cameron to be able to ride with him on some occasions. I gave my full-on expectations as this boy had already breached my trust once. So that night, I let Cameron leave with him to go spend the night, so they could go to a youth activity early the next morning.

When I picked up Cameron the next night, he immediately started to tell me how his friend had slid off the road into a ditch on the way home. It had been raining, but I would bet my last dollar the boy was going way too fast as well! I could see Cameron waiting for my response. I listened and then told him I was glad he had told me. I was, however, very disappointed that the boy's parents had not called me. They had to call a tow truck and be pulled out of the ditch… I think that any accident warrants a call from parent to parent immediately. Nonetheless, Cameron unknowingly had earned major trust points by telling me.

Wheeeeeee! Things are shifting. Yet, never quick enough for us as parents. We would like our kids to just "get it" or just "do it" because we said so. Yet, our God is faithful! He hears our prayers for our kids. He cannot make them obey us or Him, but He will continually leave the ninety-nine and go after them. He will woo their hearts.

If you had asked me a few weeks ago what would happen for school this year, I could never have imagined Cameron would chose ministry school and dual enrollment. Cameron scored 100% on his first two Old Testament quizzes. *Wheeeeeee*!

God is good. God is faithful. We must be faithful in prayer. Do not stop praying for your kids, whether they are teens or adults now. God hears our prayers! He wants our children to follow Him even more than we do. Just be faithful in praying and trusting God.

REFLECTION

Never Give Up on His Promises

We know there are many promises in God's Word. To find out how many, I did what all of you do..... I Googled it. Depending on the source, there are between 3000 – 7000 promises in the Bible. No, I did not go look at all of them, but you are welcome to do that research and then you can email me to tell me what you found.

What is important, is that we have hope because we believe God is faithful to His promises. When we experience a promise fulfilled in our life, it increases our faith, which in turn, gives us more hope. With more hope, we have more faith, which give us more hope, which builds more faith, etc. This goes on and on in our lives to bring us into a deeper walk with Him. Even in the times we may feel God is not answering or has not answered the way we had hoped, we can still rely on our past experiences of His faithfulness to bring us through.

We have circumstances in all our lives that leave us feeling out of control. That happens to be where God wants us. *"My grace is sufficient for you, for My strength is made perfect in weakness"* (2 Corinthians 12:9). He cannot work in and through us when we are trying to do it all ourselves. Sometimes, the most difficult thing, is to do nothing. We want to intervene with our children, friends, parents, boss, etc. We must pray and wait on God. Yes, I said, "Wait". Let us acknowledge that is one of the most difficult things to do in life. Second, we need to repent and ask God's forgiveness for not trusting Him and for interfering in what

He is attempting to do. We must hold onto His promises in time of waiting.

I tell Cameron he should count to ten before responding with his words. He thinks that is stupid, but little does he know, I sometimes must wait a day or so before even talking to him about something. I am counting into the thousands! Those are the times I say, "I can do all things through Christ, who strengthens me", even if those "things" includes waiting (Philippians 4:13).

The message of this chapter is that there is always HOPE in Christ. The circumstances within my home seemed impossible for me and even to some who are watching. At times, we want to *give up*, thinking there is no solution or answer. It is at those times, God wants us to *give it over* to Him so He can work in the supernatural. We must be praying expectantly. We must be watching for what He will do in someone's heart and life. What God wants to do may not be what you are expecting, but it will be so much better. He is so much wiser than we are.

You may be saying, "but you do not know my situation." You are right, I do not know your situation, but I know our God! If you could have lived here this past year, you would say, only God could do this work. We are not past all the anger and hurt, but the Holy Spirit has started a deep work in Cameron that only God can do. If I think for one moment, I can jump in and help, I am mistaken and am likely to just mess it up. There are things hidden in each of our lives that only God knows about and only the Holy Spirit can reach.

The forty days of prayer for Cameron was a starting place. The youth camps and volunteer activities were a next step. God has this, and He will lead and guide Cameron on this path. My job is to continue to love, pray, and hold on to hope though God's promises. "For we do not wrestle against flesh and blood, but against principalities, against powers, against the rulers of the darkness of this age, against spiritual hosts of wickedness in the heavenly places" (Ephesians 6:12). God has removed many of the lingering spirits we were wrestling against. That is a discussion for my next book called *Pig Pen*. It will address generational curses and things we hold onto from our past. God is faithful and He will do the work in Cameron and it will be the best work.

It is exciting and to see what God is doing and to have a first-row seat to His molding and forming in both our lives. All we need to do is be the clay. He does the work. We just need to be supple and moldable. He wants to create beauty from our ashes, give us joy for our mourning, and refine us into the purest of gold. It is His work, not ours. When we let Him, it is a beautiful work of art. When we try to tell Him how to do it or refuse to let Him change us, we become a deformed lump of clay sitting to the side of the wheel. He will let us sit there until we are ready to be supple in the Master's hand.

God is faithful! Let us place our trust and hope in Him alone.

God's Promises

Romans 12:11-12
….. not lagging in diligence, fervent in spirit, serving the Lord; rejoicing in hope, patient in tribulation, continuing steadfastly in prayer …..

2 Peter 1:4
By which have been given to us exceedingly great and precious promises, that through these you may be partakers of the divine nature, having escaped the corruption that is in the world through lust.

Isaiah 40:29-31
He gives power to the weak, and to those who have no might He increases strength. Even the youths shall faint and be weary, and the young men shall utterly fall, But those who wait on the LORD shall renew their strength; they shall mount up with wings like eagles, they shall run and not be weary, they shall walk and not faint."

Exodus 14:14
The LORD will fight for you, and you shall hold your peace.

REFLECTION QUESTIONS

What are you currently struggling with?

_____

_____

_____

_____

_____

_____

_____

_____

_____

_____

_____

_____

_____

_____

_____

_____

REFLECTION QUESTIONS

What promises had God given you?

_____

_____

_____

_____

_____

_____

_____

_____

_____

_____

_____

_____

_____

_____

_____

_____

_____

Pig
Moment 11

Looking
in to
His Eyes

Pig Moment 11
Looking In To His Eyes

The times when we are completely spent and feel like going nowhere, is usually the time we need to get up and go where we can be refilled and replenished. Even the good shifts God brings in our lives, can tire us. If you think back to those times when the Holy Spirit has filled you in a new way, it is both energizing and exhausting. God's power is so beyond what we can handle so He must change us in increments and not all at once.

It had been an emotionally exhausting week and while I felt like doing nothing come Saturday evening, I dressed and headed to King's Station for the service. The speaker that night was a prophet from our region. He spoke, wanting us to envision the glory of God in a new way. He would share a bit between worship songs. He wanted us to see the glory of God in a new and deeper way. He wanted us to visualize ourselves walking the streets of gold in heaven, but that is not where the Holy Spirit took me.

I saw a grassy field on the top of a mountain with a large tree full of leaves. Everything was green and colorful. I saw myself sitting under the tree and there was Jesus. He was sitting there facing me, reclining against the tree. I have no idea what we were discussing, but we were in conversation. I could not even see the view from the mountains, though I tried. All I could focus on was Jesus and I was drawn to look in to His blue eyes. I have no idea if Jesus really has blue eyes, but they were blue in my vision. I felt such peace in that moment. The speaker wanted us to have Jesus take us to heaven in our vision, but that just never happened. I tried to conjure that image, but kept coming back to the tree.

This past year, God was teaching me how to follow Jesus close enough to hear each word He speaks to me. I would envision myself walking so closely behind Him, that as He would lift one foot, I would step right where His foot had been. I wanted to walk in complete obedience. While sitting under that tree, God reminded me of this image that had been placed before me all year. Then in my spirit, I heard Him say, "Look in to my eyes." He told me that walking in obedience was important, but walking in love was where He wanted me to be. He showed me that I had been walking *behind* Him as a follower. He wants me to walk *with* Him as a *daughter to God the Father* and as a *bride to Christ*.

He brought dancing to my mind. If you will remember, I had an earlier vision of dancing on a field of grass with Him (Pig Moment 3). I grew up dancing and God often uses our experiences to speak to us. In couples dancing, whether it be ballroom, country or hip-hop, the two people need to be connected. The dancing term is to "hold frame." Frame is the stance of your entire body and arms for the dance. Different dances have different stances, but all require "frame" or connection to be successful. Frame is created by both dancers leaning into or pressing into each other. This pressing in, is what creates the strong connection. When there is a connection and each person holds frame, then when the male dancer leads, the woman's body will respond automatically to follow. The connection is so tight, that following is the only option.

This is what our connection to Christ should look like. He is the one leading (the husband) and we are all following (the bride). We should be leaning in to Him, while He leans in to us, so that we are constantly connected. This works in all relationships, not just our relationship with Christ. When we stay connected, things go well. As soon as one person, gets tired or weary and they "drop frame", the connection is broken or affected.

The other part of dancing we need to understand is that we are often dancing facing our partner, but going backward. The person leading is moving in a forward motion, knowing what is ahead, but we are blind to that during the dance. There will be moments when we may be moving forward and can see where we are going, but those are momentary. More importantly, we are not even looking ahead, we are looking in our partner's eyes and focused on pressing in. We learn to trust the connection for our direction.

Jesus was telling me to face Him, look in to His eyes and follow Him based on our connection. He wants me to look in to His eyes and He will lead me as I walk toward Him. God is building my faith, to walk (dance) backward, with no view of what is to come, while I was looking in to His eyes. He will lead me face-to-face. The connection is what gives me faith. When I am looking in to His eyes and staying connected, fear and worry have no place. *Wheeeeeee!*

The Holy Spirit spoke, "from this point forward, you will start each day sitting under the tree with Jesus." WOW! What a difference in how I perceived our relationship. He is now my friend; the love of my life and I will soon be His bride. I will gaze into His eyes and all other things will only be seen through what He shows me. He will lead me to the loving Father, who invites me to come crawl up in His lap as His daughter. This was enough to make this Baptist girl consider doing a Pentecostal run around the room. The introvert in me kept me from doing that, yet my heart was about to explode with joy.

Today, I was reminded of something Mama Fire said a few weeks ago (her name is Inez). She is about 80 years young and a fireball preacher. She quoted the passage, *"For now we see through a glass, darkly; but then face to face: now I know in part; but then shall I know even as also I am known"* (1 Corinthians 13:12). She talked about how in the last days, God will begin to take a cloth and wipe the glass and we will see Him more clearly. I feel like that is exactly what the Holy Spirit did for me. He wiped the glass so I could see Him face-to-face. He gave me new revelation of who He is. He gave me new insight into who I am in Him.

One thing I am learning is that God wants to show Himself to us. We just need to ask Him. Close your eyes and ask Him to show Himself to you! Be patient. I had to continue to pray and asked Him through a few worship songs and then, He gave me pictures in my mind. He will do the same for you because He loves you as if you were the only person on the planet. Seek Him, keep seeking Him and He will reveal Himself.

Some of you are wanting to know the doctrine and theology behind all this..... just rest in Him and not become anxious. I am not trying to teach doctrine here. I am talking about God touching deep down inside of you. As we enter the last days, all old wine skins must be destroyed, so get ready for things you have never imagined before (Matthew 9:17). If we cling to doctrine and spend all our time debating the finer points, we miss the relationship. We need to be rooted in the Word, and God put it simply... Love the Lord your God with ALL your heart and with ALL your soul and with ALL your strength (Deuteronomy 6:4) and love your neighbor as yourself (Matthew 22:37 and Luke 10:27). If we follow these two commands and truly love Him with ALL our heart, soul and mind, then doctrine does not need to be debated because we are all walking in Him.

For those of you who are still a bit anxious, I have verses on the "Eyes of the Lord" and seeing Him "face-to-face." Beholding the eyes of the Lord or seeing Him face-to-face does not gives us any status, they speak to who He is. These in no way make us equal to God.

> *"I am the Lord, and there is none else, there is no God beside me... a just God and a Saviour; there is none beside me. Look unto me, and be ye saved, all the ends of the earth: for I am God and there is none else."*
> Isaiah 45:1-22

Eyes of the Lord and Face to Face

I will instruct you and teach you in the way which you should go; I will counsel you with My eye upon you. Psalm 32:8

Behold, the eye of the LORD is on those who fear Him, on those who hope for His lovingkindness. Psalm 33:18

For His eyes are upon the ways of a man, And He sees all his steps. Job 34:21

For the eyes of the LORD are on the righteous, and His ears are open to their prayers... I Peter 3:12

Thus the LORD used to speak to Moses face to face, just as a man speaks to his friend When Moses returned to the camp, his servant Joshua, the son of Nun, a young man, would not depart from the tent. Exodus 33:11

Since that time no prophet has risen in Israel like Moses, whom the LORD knew face to face. Deuteronomy 34:10

The LORD spoke to you face to face at the mountain from the midst of the fire... Deuteronomy 5:4

So Jacob named the place Peniel, for he said, 'I have seen God face to face, yet my life has been preserved'. Genesis 32:30

...and they will tell it to the inhabitants of this land. They have heard that You, O LORD, are in the midst of this people, for You, O LORD, are seen eye to eye, while Your cloud stands over them; and You go before them in a pillar of cloud by day and in a pillar of fire by night. Numbers 14:14

When Gideon saw that he was the angel of the LORD, he said, Alas, O Lord GOD! For now, I have seen the angel of the LORD face to face. Judges 6:22

REFLECTION
Love and Obedience

God brings amazing people along our path to mentor and help direct us. There is wisdom and safety in a multitude of counselors according to Proverbs 11:14 and 15:22. Yet, man's opinions never supersede God's omniscience. The person we need to rely on for answers is the Holy Spirit. Too often, we are looking to those around us for direction. When you have a situation that is stressful or something you need help with, what do you do first? Do you post it on Facebook, text several friends for advice, complain about the situation or person, or do you first run to God?

If you were to stop and think, your friends generally do not have answers for their own lives, so why do we think they will have wisdom for our lives? Even those closest to us, who love us, and want the best for us, do not know God's best plan for our lives. God will place specific people on your path to help you and guide you. You will know they have divine wisdom when they point you back to God.

Just as in the short vision God gave me, the answer lies in looking in to His eyes and meeting Him face-to-face. I used to need to talk to someone I could physically see in front of me or someone whose voice I could hear on the phone. Yet, the person with all the answers and the right answers is always with me even though I cannot physically touch Him. I can close my eyes and then look in to His eyes. I can close my eyes and see Him face-to-face.

In the past few months, I had a few situations that I took to God and told no one. After the situation occurred and I wrote about it, one of my proof readers told me she had no idea and wished I would have called her so she could pray with and for me. I told her, I needed to tell no one. I needed God to show up and I needed to know it was Him and Him alone working in the situation. (Don't applaud me, I am still learning and it is only by His grace I did this).

We all have an inner need for love and acceptance. We often seek it out from those we can physically touch and see. God is now giving me the ability to touch and see Him when I close my eyes. Jesus is becoming my best friend. The one I want to talk to first and last. The one whose opinion matters most. I have moved from the servant, walking behind Him to a friend who can see Him face-to-face.

> *No longer do I call you servants, for a servant does not know what his master is doing; but I have called you friends, for all things that I heard from My Father I have made known to you.* John 15:15

However, we do not move into the role of friend without believing His Word. We demonstrate our belief by our obedience to His Word. *"Abraham believed God, and it was counted to him as righteousness" and he was called a friend of God"* (James 2:23, Galatians 3:6, Romans 4:3, and Genesis 15:6). Did Abraham just believe and never act? NO! He had to walk out that belief. When God told Abraham, he would have a child, there were actions he had to take for that to become reality. Abraham believed God and obeyed and then he was called a friend of God. He believed God to have the son of promise and then he believed for his son's life on Mount Moriah (Genesis 22). Both times, his belief required obedience.

It begins with our belief and is followed by our obedience. As we walk in obedience, we draw closer to Him and knowing His heart. We begin to fall in love with who He is. We begin to want to spend more and more time with Him. Knowing His heart and seeking Him, not what He can do for us, is what moves us from obedient servant to friend.

Think of your best friend. How do you act when you are with that person? Do you show honor and respect or do you treat him or her unkindly? Do you listen when he or she speaks or is it always about you? How we view our earthly friendships will often be an indication of our view of a friendship with God. He does not see things as we do and His view of friendship is much deeper than ours. His thoughts are not our thoughts and His ways are not our ways (Isaiah 55: 8-9).

Would you jump in front of a bullet for your best friend? Would you go after the alligator that has just grabbed them? (I live in Florida – this could happen). I think of my best friend, whom I have known for over 40 years. I believe I would take a bullet for her and I definitely would go after a gator (I hate gators). Then, I have a few other friends that are close, but not as close as my BFF. Would I do that for them? What about the person I know and may call a friend, but we really do not hang out or call each other to chat? The person on the next level of my friend list. Would I risk my life for that person?

Greater love has no one than this, that someone lay down his life for his friends (John 15:13).

God's nature is all-in. He gives all, in every situation. Can you imagine? He leaves the ninety-nine for the one. He gave His one and only Son for us. So, before you jump to saying, "Jesus is my friend", consider the cost. He does not take friendship lightly, as we often do. Moving from servant to friend is not just moving to a face-to-face status, it is moving to a deeper love. It is not a status we achieve, it is a relationship.

Too often, religion looks to create status. You hear this in discussions about the different leadership positions one holds, the ministry they lead, or the gifts they believe they have been given. God cares more about the relationship, than any of that. He is not about titles, He is about changing people's lives. This comes about as we encounter His love in ways we have never encountered Him before.

God is HOLY and JUST. We need an awareness that we are in the presence of this almighty, holy God who will hold each of us accountable for our thoughts, motives, actions and words. Because of our sin nature, we do not naturally seek to honor God. We seek out things that gratify us, rather than things that glorify God. If we deny this fact, then we are living in a lie and pride. The Godliest people I know, will tell you just how wretched they are and how they need God every day to walk in Him.

God's love is what ultimately woos us to want to come closer to Him. However, understanding who He is and His holiness is where it begins. *"The fear of the Lord is the*

BEGINNING of wisdom and the knowledge of the Holy One is understanding" (Proverbs 9:10). There are some out there that would say, that is does not mean fear and they will quote, "perfect love cast our fear." Yes, PERFECT love does cast out fear, but that is not where we start with God. His love is perfect, but ours is not. I love what Bill Johnson says, "fear means fear." Just His presence should put us on our faces. The Bible says, "every knee will bow" at the name of Jesus. We should live in such awe of who He is and understanding He is holy. God cannot even look on us except through the blood of His son.

David prayed, *"Teach me thy way, O Lord; I will walk in thy truth: unite my heart to fear thy name"* (Psalm 86:11).

II Corinthians 5:10
For we must all appear before the judgment seat of Christ; that everyone may receive the things done in his body, according to that he hath done, whether it be good or bad.

Philippians 2:10-12
That at the name of Jesus every knee should bow, of things in heaven, and things in earth, and things under the earth; and that every tongue should confess that Jesus Christ is Lord, to the glory of God the Father. Wherefore, my beloved, as ye have always obeyed, not as in my presence only, but now much more in my absence, work out your own salvation with fear and trembling.

Isaiah 45:1-22
I am the Lord, and there is none else, there is no God beside me....I am the Lord, and there is none else....and there is no God else beside me; a just God and a Saviour; there is none beside me. Look unto me, and be ye saved, all the ends of the earth: for I am God and there is none else.

Proverbs 22:4
By humility and the fear of the Lord are riches, and honor, and life.

Our relationship with God begins with fear and understanding He is holy. As we come closer to Him, the love grows more and more like His perfect love. I loved my dad as a little girl, but I also had a very healthy fear of him. Not that he would hurt me, but that I would disappoint him and I also knew he would bring correction when I did something that was outside of what he was trying to teach me.

Some of you have been walking with God for years, but have not really encountered His love. You may even have some of the gifts of the spirit and still not have ever felt like you had a love encounter with Him. You can have that today! You can start to track your very own "pig moments" with Him. Just ask Him to reveal His love to you in a new way today. Ask Him to encounter you with His love. Pray, keep praying, listen and wait. He WILL encounter you. He must, to be true to who He is and His Word.

Some of you reading this may not have even come to know Him as your Father. Maybe, you have lived not knowing who He is at all. You might have been taught He is an angry God waiting to punish you. Maybe, you never learned about God's love for you. You might have grown up hearing about Jesus, who walked among men. Jesus is the brother and a friend. God loved you so much that He sacrificed His only son for you. Jesus loved you so much, that He willing, laid down His life for you.

HOW TO MEET GOD

If you have never accepted God's love into your life, you can do that now. Read the verses below.

Romans 3:23 *For all have sinned, and come short of the glory of God.*

Romans 6:23 *For the wages of sin is death; but the gift of God is eternal life through Jesus Christ our Lord.*

Romans 5:8 *But God demonstrates His own love toward us, in that while we were still sinners, Christ died for us.*

Romans 10:9 *If you confess with your mouth Jesus as Lord, and believe in your heart that God raised Him from the dead, you will be saved.*

Romans 10:13 *For everyone who calls on the name of the Lord will be saved.*

Romans 5:1 *Therefore, since we have been justified through faith, we have peace with God through our Lord Jesus Christ*

Romans 8:1 *Therefore, there is now no condemnation for those who are in Christ Jesus.*

You can ask Him to be the Lord of your life by simply talking to Him in prayer.

God, I ask you to reveal yourself to me right now. I understand I have broken your laws and sinned against you. I ask you to forgive me for sinning against you. Thank you for sending Jesus to die for my sins. I give you my life and ask you to become Lord. Thank you for saving me and giving me life eternal and heaven. Amen.

Remember Your Pig Moments

My journey of *Pig Moments* span from March 2017 to July 2018. God has been so faithful and has done such a deep work in me in a short seventeen months. I pray this journey of *Pig Moments* we have shared, will help you to think about the miracles in your own life.

We must make a conscious effort to REMEMBER all He has done. It is so easy to move from one miracle to the next problem and forget. We often wonder how the Children of Israel could cross the Red Sea on dry ground, be fed manna daily, or follow a cloud by day and then not trust God. We criticize them for building idols and worshiping a golden calf. Yet, we do the same. It may not look like a large golden calf in the middle of our living room, but we are placing all sorts of things in front of Him. We are praising Him one day from the mountain top experience and the next day He can find us wallowing in self-pity in the desert.

My story is not special. GOD HAS WRITTEN THE STORY OF YOUR LIFE as well. Seek it out by seeking Him. Start writing down the miracles God gives you, so you can read what He has done in the past and walk in faith and hope when you are doing through the desert.

Whether you like to type like me, or prefer to handwrite in a journal, I implore you to begin the journey. Praise is one of the most powerful ways to stay in His will and keep the enemy at bay. We can praise Him more easily when we look back over the history of His faithfulness. Think of the legacy you can leave for your children and grandchildren. The Israelites piled stones up in remembrance. We may not create piles of stones in our yard, but we can track God's goodness in our lives and leave that legacy for others.

God is worthy of our praise. He is worthy of our honor. He is worthy to be remembered for His faithfulness. Start letting Him write His story through you today. Write it. Read it. Share it. Rejoice in it. You too can start finding reasons in each day to yell WHEEEEEEE at the top of your voice.

May you have many Wheeeeeee moments in your future!

This little piggy encountered Jesus,
This little piggy experienced miracles,
This little piggy has peace and joy,
This little piggy expects victories,
And this little piggy praised Him by singing
"wee wee wee" all the way home.

The
End...

Just
the
Beginning
of your
Journey

References

Batterson, M. (2006). *In a Pit with a Lion on a Snowy Day*. Colorado Springs, CO: Multnomah Books.

Herman, D. (2007). The Cambridge Companion to Narrative. Cambridge University Press. p. 9.

Patterson, K., Grenny, J., McMillan, R. and Switzler, A. (2011). Crucial conversations: Tools for talking when stakes are high. (2nd ed.). Vital Smarts. As cited in Meier, J.D. 6 Styles Under Stress. Sources of Insight. Retrieved from http://sourcesofinsight.com/six-styles-under-stress/

Tozer, A. W. (1978). *The Knowledge of the Holy Spirit*. San Francisco, CA: Harper.

OTHER WORKS

Detours: That Become Life's Paths

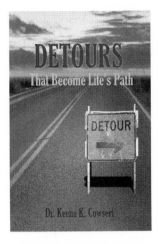

DETOURS is a testament to God's faithfulness in our circumstances. This book is a collection of true stories that show God's grace and mercy. It will challenge anyone willing go on this journey, to find God in their circumstances. This is God's invitation for you to allow Him to walk with you on your DETOURS. It is God's inviation to find the path where He can lead you to a secure and exciting life in Him.

COMING SOON . . . .

Pig Pen

God rescues us from sin and the Pig Pen. We do all we can to walk in His calling. Yet, we often find ourselves struggling. Could it be that there are still remnants of mud left from the Pig Pen? We may be wearing the Father's robe, but underneath is still some mud that has not been washed off. This book examines how to wash off all the mud and allow God to write your new story.

Unmasked

Unmasked examines the masks that we wear to disguise our weaknesses, protect ourselves from hurt in life or to perform for acceptance from others. It examines the defense mechanisms designed to hide the person hiding behind the mask. This book will show how to remove the masks, so you can start to walk in the person that God designed YOU to be.

Counseling, Life Coaching and Inner Healing

If you need someone to talk to you can contact Dr. K. You can Skype, Facetime, or do a phone session. All sessions are Biblically based in Christ Jesus. Counseling and Life Coaching are solution-focused and short term (2-6 sessions). Inner Healing sessions are based on the Holy Spirit's work in you.

You can contact Dr. K through the website and she will contact you within 48 hours.

Healing for Hearts

Email: **Info@DKcommunity.org**

Website: **www.DKcommunity.org**

Areas of specialty:
- Depression/Anxiety
- Relationship Struggles & Setting Boundaries
- Emotional Fatigue
- Child and Teen Support Sessions
- Religious Struggles
- Ministry or Church Staff Support Sessions
- Pastor's Wives Support Sessions

ABOUT THE AUTHOR

Dr. Keena K. Cowsert is a college professor by day and a ministry leader by night. She has a Master's Degree in Speech Communication with a focus on Organizational Training and Development. Her Doctorate of Education is in Community and Pastoral Counseling. Dr. K teaches Public Speaking for local colleges and online graduate courses for Liberty University's Care and Community Counseling Department.

Dr. K is a key-note speaker for conferences and other events. She has led several ministries over the years including: singles, Celebrate Recovery, and women's ministry. Dr. K is the founder and director of DK Community (Daughters of the King), a non-profit organization under Galatians 6:2 (www.g62.info). DK Community focuses on women's conferences, Christian art galas, leadership training, discipleship training and Women of Worship nights.

She is passionate about ministry and leading others to a deeper walk in Christ. In her free time, she likes walks on the beach, having coffee with friends and playing with her dogs.

For more information or to schedule Dr. K to speak or bring an event to your area, contact her at:

Email   **Info@DKcommunity.org**
Website   **www.DKcommunity.org**

RESOURCES

Graphic Designs by
Dianne Steele Graphic Designs
Dianne.Steele@gmail.com

Web Designs by
Ann & Mike Gervasio
3 Strand Creations
http://www.3strandscreations.com
3strandscreations@gmail.com

Made in the USA
Columbia, SC
22 July 2019